Mountain Weather

A Guide for Skiers and Hillwalkers

• William Burroughs •

The Crowood Press

First published in 1995 by
The Crowood Press Ltd
Ramsbury, Marlborough
Wiltshire SN8 2HR

This impression 1996

British Library Cataloguing-in-Publication Data
A catalogue record for this book is available from the British Library.

ISBN 1 85223 877 1

Dedication
To Suzanne, my skiing companion.

Picture Credits
All line-drawings by Bob Constant

Acknowledgements
I am indebted to a number of people who have helped me, both by providing
information and supplying many of the pictures that appear in this book. These
include: Christine Berni, U Liebing and A Roth at the Institute for Snow and
Avalanche Research in Weissfluhjoch; B Baylis and N Lonie at the University of
Dundee; John Yates-Smith and Fiona Easdale at YSE Limited; D Kerindi at
Nevica; J-L Costerg, J Nell and J Perroud of the Technical Services in Val d'Isere;
Derek Elsom and Mary Spence at Weather; and D Bennetts, F Fliri, J Minhinick,
C Pfister, T Oke, S Reber and M Schuepp.

Typeset by Acorn Bookwork, Salisbury, Wiltshire
Printed and bound in Great Britain

Contents

Preface

The genesis of this book was a Christmas holiday spent in Val d'Isère in 1987. The local newspapers at the time were full of pictures of bare ski-slopes and one in particular was the source of great merriment, showing a narrow ribbon of man-made snow running across a lowly meadow in Samedan near St Moritz. By comparison, the extensive snow my family and I were enjoying was heaven, although there was dangerous crust off piste, and the piste was a bit thin in places. Even so, Val d'Isère was in a different world compared to the barren slopes described in the newspapers. And this is what set me wondering why the conditions could be so different across relatively short distances.

In subsequent years, while digging out evidence for the causes of these differences between resorts and mountain ranges, I never ceased to be amazed at how little attention people paid to climatological data. I met friends who had had disastrous Christmas holidays in Kitzbühel, when, as keen skiers, they well knew that the chances of good snow were slim. At the same time, the stock of published snow reports plummeted as many skiers learnt to their cost that what they found in the mountains fell far short of what they had been led to expect.

This difference in conditions in the Alps resulted in an understandable mad rush to North America, which offers a huge range of options and experiences. It does, however, also have dramatic fluctuations from winter to winter, so without an adequate knowledge of what can reasonably be expected, there is a real risk that you could spend a lot more money and time in travelling only to get conditions that are no better than in Europe. The absence of a readily available source of information which could allow holiday-makers to assess the options makes a lottery of any decision.

Clearly, therefore, there was a need to provide more information about what weather could be expected in the mountains. The snowier seasons of recent years in the Alps have not altered this situation. Indeed, the continued tragic loss of life among skiers and hillwalkers in avalanches and storms has further underlined that it is vital to know how the weather can influence our enjoyment of activities in the mountains.

With all this in mind, I have sought to pull together as much data as possible to enable you to form a view on the balance of risk. This does involve quite a lot of statistics, but you should not be put off by these as the text provides a summary of their implications, thus making the figures more accessible. If the conclusions drawn in these pages prove to be at odds with what you were expecting, then by delving deeper you should be further illuminated and, hopefully, rewarded. In essence, the purpose of this book is to increase the odds that you find the combination of sun and snow you are looking for, and do not end up paddling around on a tiny, overcrowded, rock-strewn strip of slush with a bunch of fellow losers.

1

Introduction

Great things are done when men and mountains meet;
This is not done by jostling in the street.
William Blake (1757–1827)

Mountains have always been seen as awe-inspiring. Regarded as the home of gods and evil spirits by those who lived in their shadow, over the centuries they have lured hardy souls to confront the challenge they represent. Following on the heels of those intrepid pioneers who first conquered the peaks came a swelling flood of enthusiasts who fell in love with the mountains. This flood has now become a torrent, and an increasing proportion of visitors are taking on the mountains when they are at their most dangerous – in winter. In these realms of snow and ice the weather plays a major part in defining the scale of the challenge, and yet to the vast majority of those who venture into the mountains, meteorology is a closed book. However, with some knowledge of how the weather affects their enjoyment and safety, enthusiasts could get so much more out of their visits; furthermore, they could avoid the ever-present dangers – about 150 people are killed by avalanches each year in the Alps alone.

This book will explore those aspects of the weather that are relevant to people who enjoy sporting activities in the mountains. While the principal focus is on the winter half of the year (November to April in the northern hemisphere) and, in particular, to the needs of skiers, many of the elements described are also of direct relevance to hillwalking, climbing and other sporting activities. Nor is the coverage just for those who know the mountains well; family skiing holidays are just as vulnerable to bad weather, and the choice of where and when to go is no less important than for the more adventurous. The objective of the book, therefore, is to provide a balanced coverage of the meteorological aspects for anyone who seeks to enjoy mountain snow and ice.

WHICH MOUNTAINS?

Mountains cover roughly one-fifth of the land surface of the Earth, stretching across every continent and extending from the South Pole to northern Greenland. On the highest mountains at the Equator and at virtually every other latitude there are permanent snowfields and glaciers. There are dedicated climbers, skiers and walkers who live close to many of these ranges and get out to them every weekend; equally, dedicated enthusiasts will travel half-way round the world to scale particular peaks or ski fabled runs when the conditions are right. But for all mountain-lovers – whether they are weekend climbers in Athens, skiers in Vancouver getting out on their local slopes or Britons jetting to Utah to enjoy a week of champagne powder – the right weather is central to their enjoyment. As such a vast range of localities makes the provision of useful specific advice impossible, the only answer is to concentrate on certain parts of the world and seek to draw general messages from the specific results obtained in these localities.

To start with, what exactly are mountains? Geographers have debated this subject for many years, but perhaps the most useful definition here is the one that states that 'high mountains' have an upper tree-line and a snow-line, with sufficient snow to produce distinctive glacial landforms. In northern Scandinavia this would include anything above a few hundred metres, in northern Britain it would include slopes above about 500m (1,500ft) and in the Alps it would include peaks above about 1,500m (5,000ft). In North America these 'high mountains' would range from close to a few hundred metres in height in the coastal ranges of Alaska and British Columbia, to around 3,000m (10,000ft) in the southern Rockies of Colorado and New Mexico. Further south, in the Andes, the level rises to around 4,500m (15,000ft) at the Equator and descends to a few hundred metres in southern Chile.

In addition, we need to include in our definition the hilly areas below the tree-line that have reliable snow cover during winter and spring, as these are used by skiers. This will also extend our definition to include mountains which do not rise above the tree-line – as on the east coast of North America. Thus we find that our definition of mountains includes peaks from Norway to New Zealand, and from Alaska to Patagonia.

When it comes to obtaining detailed studies of mountain weather, the scope is limited as many areas have not been the subject of extensive measurements, despite the fact that they are relatively accessible. Inevitably,

many lessons have to be drawn from work that has been carried out in the Alps, the Rockies or the uplands of the British Isles. In addition, many of the measurements taken were made for purposes unrelated to current interests in leisure activities. Although some work was purely curiosity-driven research, much of it was for economic reasons. So, while there has been research in support of tourism development since the 1960s, prior to this period it was driven by the needs of construction safety, forestry and hydrology. Although this information was not geared to the needs of the leisure industries, it does, however, contain much useful information. But the fact that most of this work has been done in the Alps at places like the Swiss Institute for Snow and Avalanche Research at Weissfluhjoch above Davos means that there will inevitably be a European flavour to the book. None the less, the aim will be to show that what is true for the Alps is also applicable to high mountains in other parts of the world.

WHAT ACTIVITIES?

The principal focus of the book will be on those sports that rely on snow and ice during the winter half of the year. The assumption is that anyone taking an active holiday in the mountains during winter will wish to enjoy the magical transformation brought about by snow and ice; from the magnificent scenery to the challenge of steep snowfields or sheer icefalls, these are the ingredients that lure winter-sports enthusiasts to the mountains. Whether it is gentle langlauf (Nordic skiing) in snow-draped forests, or leaping off sheer cliffs and descending 60-degree slopes on skis, the amount and quality of the snow is central to the enjoyment.

The meteorological elements that produce the right conditions for maximum enjoyment of these activities are snow and sunshine in roughly equal measure. Although some activities can still be enjoyed without an adequate supply of one or other of these essential ingredients, most people hope to get the right balance. So, while winter climbers do not depend too heavily on these conditions and parapenters on skis can take off on a short strip of slush and land on nursery slopes of artificial snow, most of us go for the right mixture of sun and snow. In this context the demands of skiers are greatest. It makes sense, therefore, to concentrate on these needs and then show that what matters to skiers is relevant – to a greater or lesser extent – to all the other activities. In so doing, I intend to show that this rationalization is not borne from the fact that, as a skiing addict, whose nearest contact with real mountaineering is to peer out of the observation window on the North Wall of the Eiger in disbelief, I cannot see beyond the needs of the skiing fraternity. Instead, my aim is to show that the demanding requirements of the skiing majority effectively cover most of the needs of other sports, and where they do not, it is a simple matter to extend the coverage accordingly.

WHY THE WEATHER MATTERS

Anyone who enjoys time in the mountains will recognize that every aspect of the upland environment mirrors the climate. From the very rocks, riven by the action of snow, ice and wind, through the graduation of vegetation with altitude, to isolated trees at the treeline, whose branches like flags proclaim the direction of the prevailing wind, the signs of the weather are everywhere.

Equally, winter activities in the mountains are dominated by the weather. I have already touched on the high death toll in the Alps,

but consider the fact that in the Scottish Highlands, accidents, many of which are weather-related, kill more people than die on the region's roads. The same tragic story is repeated in other parts of the world. It is not just the immediate hazards of venturing out in difficult conditions that matter, for huge sums of money have been invested in many countries to develop the winter-sports potential of mountainous areas on the assumption that the climate will not change appreciably. On every timescale, therefore, a better knowledge of how weather should enter into our plans can make all the difference between success and failure. From making long-term investment decisions about building resorts or investing in property, to buying clothing and choosing the right time and place for a family holiday, or what to do on a specific day, the weather enters our calculations.

In essence, learning more about mountain weather is a form of risk analysis: some risk is an essential element of the challenge of the mountains, but it must be tempered by realism. For example, anyone wishing to ski off piste after a heavy fall of snow knows the dangers, but what they have to decide, in the light of local knowledge, is when it is sensible to go in search of deep new snow and when it is best to avoid it. Similarly, decisions on when and where to take mountain holidays are bound to be influenced by what we know about the climate of the region. Those who are blissfully unaware of the substantial differences between the snow and temperature records of different resorts cannot be surprised if they find that their choice has fared badly compared to better endowed resorts.

It pays to know how the weather can affect what you do in the mountains, whether it be from minute to minute, or over the years. This involves identifying which meteorological elements really matter, and where better to start than with snow?

2
Snow

I love snow, and all the forms
Of the radiant frost.
Percy Bysshe Shelley (1792–1822)

Snow is what attracts people to the mountains in the winter. While the other features of mountains – breath-taking scenery, exhilarating walking and fresh air – are important, without snow most people are desolate and skiers are frustrated beyond measure. So, mountain weather in winter has to start with snow. In order to find good snow it helps to know how it is formed, what happens to it once it has settled on the ground and how it changes with time.

WHAT IS SNOW?

When asked to define snow, most people will say that it is frozen rain. If asked to draw a picture of a snowflake they will, however, draw a delicate hexagonal shape that does not resemble frozen rain in the least. Clearly, there is a gap in many people's understanding of how snow is formed and what it looks like.

On rare occasions at high altitudes and in the right conditions, snowflakes will actually fall as beautifully symmetrical hexagonal crystals, just the way we imagine them and just like the pictures published in so many physics books (*see* Fig 2.1). For the rest of the time, however, snow falls in a wide variety of forms, ranging from fine, pitty grains to large, fluffy lumps of 'cotton wool' that result

Fig 2.1 *Everyone's image of snow – a star-shaped hexagonal (dendritic) crystal. (Reproduced with permission of the Institute for Snow and Avalanche Research, Weissfluhjoch.)*

in rapid accumulations of deep, wet snow. Snow can fall at virtually any temperature below 0°C (32°F) and even at higher temperatures, but the proportion of snow to rain falls off rapidly above 3°C (37°F). As skiers know only too well, the type of snow makes all the difference to the snowpack, even before it starts to age. So, while it is the subject of philological dispute as to whether the Inuit have twenty-nine different words to describe snow, the English language has its own glossary – ranging from 'champagne powder' to 'Sierra cement' or 'porridge' – to reflect the ups and downs of skiing.

Snow Formation

To understand why snow comes in so many forms requires a little physics. It may come as a surprise to many readers that theories about the physical processes that form rain and snow are still the subject of debate. The basic problem lies in explaining why some clouds produce rain and snow, while seemingly identical looking ones do not. The answer lies in the fact that for water droplets or ice crystals to form in a cloud they have to have a surface on which they can condense, or crystallize; they cannot simply condense or crystallize in mid-air out of nothing. Such surfaces are readily available in the form of dust and other particles in the atmosphere, but how rapidly condensation or crystalliza-tion occurs depends on the nature of the particles' surfaces and their size. In most cases these particles are not suitable for forming ice crystals. As a consequence, clouds whose temperatures are below freezing contain a mixture of ice crystals and water droplets. Supercooled water droplets can exist at temperatures as low as $-40°C$ ($-40°F$) before they crystallize spontaneously.

At levels in the atmosphere where the temperature is below freezing, ice crystals and snowflakes grow by means of two processes. First, because water molecules can evaporate more easily from water droplets than they can sublime from ice crystals, there is a steady flow of water vapour from droplets to crystals. Also, as small droplets evaporate more rapidly than big ones, the average size of the water droplets increases as the cloud ages. The process of vapour flux means that the ice crystals build up quickly at the expense of water droplets to form a variety of exotic crystalline forms (*see* Fig 2.2). Incidentally, it

Fig 2.2   *A collection of snow crystals, showing that they come in many shapes and sizes.*
(*Reproduced with permission of the Institute for Snow and Avalanche Research,*
Weissfluhjoch.)

is this process that led atmospheric physicists to conclude that if clouds were seeded with artificial freezing nuclei, it would make them precipitate more efficiently. However, after forty-five years of weather-modification experiments using substances such as silver iodide, there is still no convincing evidence that this process increases the amount of rain or snow produced. This failure is a measure of how little is known about the precise details of ice-crystal formation in clouds.

The second process is easier to appreciate. Ice crystals grow by bumping into each other and colliding with water droplets (*see* Fig 2.3). Also, when larger supercooled droplets freeze, they do so from the outside, and so when the core freezes the subsequent expansion causes the droplet to shatter into random shards of ice. This explains why so many snowflakes have complicated and amorphous forms – indeed, large snowflakes can contain a hundred or more individual crystals that have clumped together during repeated collisions within the clouds. Furthermore, if the flakes then fall below freezing level in the cloud and start to melt, only to be swept aloft by updraughts, they can form soft hail or hail as they go through this process of accretion while melting and freezing several times.

All this helps to explain why snowflakes come in so many shapes and sizes, and also why it is so difficult to predict precisely how much and in what form snow will fall. It is, however, possible to make some observations about the conditions that produce specific types of snow. Laboratory measurements show that at different temperatures and humidities only certain types of crystals are formed. The conditions for forming the fine hexagonal, dendritic crystals are temperatures between −12°C (10°F) and −16°C (3°F); at higher or lower temperatures a variety of prisms, columns or plates are formed. But in real clouds these distinctions are of

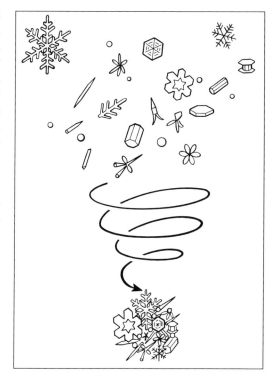

Fig 2.3   *A diagram showing how mixing in clouds causes many forms of ice crystals and supercooled water droplets to combine to form complex snowflakes.*

little concern as the vertical motion of the air means that crystals experience a wide range of temperatures and air of different temperatures is often mixed vigorously. This means that accretion by collision is the most common process and snowflakes consist of a mixture of crystals of different forms fractured and fused to produce complex structures.

Where clouds are not forced to rise rapidly by mountains or by vigorous weather systems, there is a greater chance that more fine crystals will form – thus the formation of high-quality powder snow is more likely in continental interiors, such as the area between the Sierra Nevada and the Rockies.

Here, the chances of more stable cloud systems occurring are even higher and often their temperatures are suited to forming dendritic crystals. Also, the fact that the air has crossed high, arid, dusty and salty plains means that it has a higher concentration of freezing nuclei on which ice crystals can form. This may explain why Utah has an unrivalled reputation for fine powder snow.

Conversely, where moist maritime air is forced to rise rapidly and produces heavy snowfall, it is not surprising that this often consists of big, wet, aggregated flakes. Not only are there more flakes to bump into each other, but the presence of water droplets helps fuse them together. However, measurements have shown that the proportion of different types of crystal and the amount of water droplets varies appreciably over a few kilometres. No wonder, with such variations, that it is not possible to draw any hard and fast rules about the water equivalent of snow depths. In good powder, the equivalent of 1cm (0.4in) of rainfall will be 15–20cm (6–8in) of snow, but with heavy, wet conditions the same amount of water will produce only 4cm (1.6in) of sticky snow.

It follows from this description that the amount of vapour in the air is crucial to how much snow can be formed. Since there is nearly five times more vapour in saturated air at 0°C (32°F) than in saturated air at −20°C (−4°F), the heaviest snowfall is likely to occur at temperatures close to freezing point. However, there is still considerable moisture to be wrung out of cold, rising air. Since vertical motion is a major component of weather systems great and small – from thunderstorms to the largest depressions – snowfall can occur at temperatures well below freezing. Furthermore, snow can be swept aloft to much colder levels or carried long distances to colder areas. There is no shortage of instances of driving snowstorms at temperatures well below −20°C (−4°F), as anyone who lives in North Dakota or Novosibirsk, or who works in the high resorts of the Alps or the Rockies can testify. So, the quaint British notion that 'it is too cold to snow' has little place in meteorology in general, and mountain meteorology in particular. All it tells us is that the weather situation which combines heavy snow and very low temperatures hardly ever happens in Hertfordshire or Herefordshire.

SNOWPACK

The process of vapour transport that underlies the formation of snowflakes is central to changes that take place in the snowpack. However, on the ground it is not the flow from water droplets to ice crystals that matters, but rather from warmer to colder layers.

Conditions Below the Surface

In deep snow the temperature gradient between the ground and the top of the snow controls how much vapour flows through the pack, where it is most likely to recrystallize, or whether it will escape to the atmosphere. Frequently, the temperature of the snow in contact with the ground is at or only just below 0°C (32°F); in contrast, the temperature at the surface fluctuates continually. On bright sunny days, or when the air temperature is above freezing point, the surface snow will be at 0°C (32°F). In very cold, clear, calm conditions, the surface temperature will fall well below the air temperature a metre or so above the snow because snow is a highly efficient radiator of heat.

The diurnal fluctuations in temperature, together with the variations of the weather from day to day, cause the flux of water vapour through the snowpack to change con-

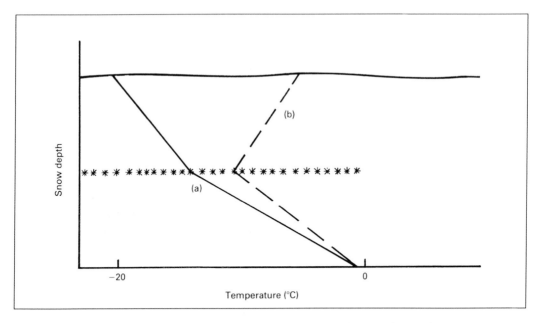

Fig 2.4 *The temperature gradient through the snowpack, showing how this depends not only on the difference between the temperature of the air and the ground and the varying properties of the intervening snowpack, but also on the time of day. At night, when the air above the snow is very cold (a), the gradient can be completely different from when the air warms up around noon (b).*

tinually (*see* Fig 2.4). Moreover, depending on the density of the snow at different levels, the temperature gradient and its porosity will both vary. So, the changes that the snow undergoes are complex and mostly hidden from view. This metamorphosis assumes a number of forms. First, the snow may lose its crystalline structure rapidly and become granular or amorphous in appearance (*see* Fig 2.5). This change can occur when there is no significant temperature gradient in the new snowpack. For this reason, and also because it leads to a degradation of the snow quality, the process is known as either **equitempera-ture metamorphosis** or **destructive meta-morphosis**. The pace at which these changes occur depends principally on the temperature of the snow – the colder it is the slower the rate of change.

The second change sees the grains fusing together, the degree of binding within the pack depending on the temperature and original condition of the snow. Again, the colder and drier the conditions, the slower the change in the snow. This means that deep falls of powder snow on shady slopes subjected to prolonged cold spells will remain unstable for many days. The risk of powder avalanches (*see* page 81) in these conditions will therefore last far longer than the two or three days usually thought to be sufficient to stabilize a new fall of snow. Conversely, any thawing will accelerate the process, with the pack consolidating rapidly; this process is sometimes called **melt metamorphosis**.

Where new snow fuses together rapidly to form a consolidated layer, a third process comes into play. The interface between snow

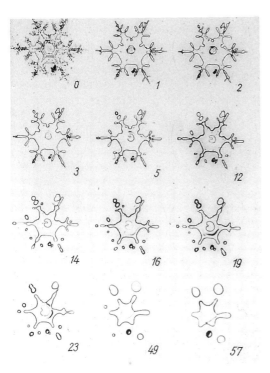

Fig 2.5   A series of pictures showing how the shape of a single snow crystal in a closed atmosphere degrades over time. (Reproduced with permission of the Institute for Snow and Avalanche Research, Weissfluhjoch.)

Fig 2.6   Depth hoar. An example of the plate-like crystals of ice which can build up in the snowpack and weaken the bonding between different layers of snow. (Reproduced with permission of the Institute for Snow and Avalanche Research, Weissfluhjoch.)

of different ages can become the point at which vapour prefers to recrystallize, and this can lead to the formation of plate-like crystals – **depth hoar** (*see* Fig 2.6) – which are capable of weakening and effectively lubricating the bond between the two layers. It may be many days or even weeks before this process has run its course, so the fact that the snowpack appears to have settled down without producing any slab avalanches after heavy snowfall (*see* page 81) does not mean that it will remain safe – beneath the surface the continual hidden process of change goes on. Moreover, the fact that the snowpack is so sensitive to both fluctuations in the weather and changes

within its various layers makes it fiendishly difficult to anticipate when a given slope will become unsafe. As a general rule, the greater the temperature difference between the ground and the surface, the greater the vapour flux up through the snow. This means that in calm, cold conditions the changes in the snowpack can be substantial, and explains why the avalanche risk can increase rapidly during very cold spells.

We shall return to the problem of avalanche prediction in Chapter 7, but for the moment it is important to understand that it is impossible to form an accurate impression of what is going on below the surface merely

Fig 2.7 *A snowpit, showing the different layers in the snow. (Reproduced with permission of the Institute for Snow and Avalanche Research, Weissfluhjoch.)*

Surface Conditions

On the surface, the changes are much easier to see. Lovers of powder know only too well how quickly a firm crust can form on new snow, even in cold, clear conditions. When the air temperature rises above freezing this process accelerates rapidly and, if combined with rain followed by freezing weather, then in no time we have **boiler plate**, so beloved of skiers on the east coast of the United States. On prepared pistes the efforts of the grooming machines can overcome all but the worst conditions, but it is a different story off piste. Furthermore, unwary climbers and walkers are particularly vulnerable in these conditions – even on a relatively gentle slope a slip can lead to a dangerous uncontrolled slide or fall if you have nothing to slow you down. Even more treacherous is where melt water flows over exposed rocky surfaces and then freezes to form a thin layer of ice, known as 'verglas'. All this means it is vital when on snow and ice for walkers to carry an ice axe and know how to use it in the event of a fall (clear instructions appear in many mountain guides – *see* Further Reading). In principle, skiers are better equipped, although in practice arresting one's descent after a fall on an icy crust using ski edges and poles is easier said than done. One thing is certain, however, and that is that it is folly to dispense with gloves in the warm sunshine when skiing on such crust. The surface is like sandpaper and you will only leave a lot of skin behind if you attempt to stop a fall with your bare hands.

There is one other interesting surface effect, this being the formation of ice crystals during a prolonged dry, cold spell. In extreme cases in sheltered sites, the crystals can grow up to 10cm (4in) in length, like fine leaves protruding from the snow. On the slopes this **surface hoar** is more normally

by inspecting from above and studying recent weather changes. It *is* possible to form a clear view of the stability of the local snowpack by digging a pit (*see* Fig 2.7), but this fact is only of limited value to anyone travelling considerable distances in the mountains as the nature of strong and weak layers may vary considerably from place to place. So, while digging a snowpit is excellent education for the dedicated ski tourer, what really matters is making decisions about how to tackle routes across potentially risky slopes, and here there is no real substitute for local expertise.

about 1cm (0.4cm) long and looks like delicate sintered petals. As such, the crystals are pleasing to the eye and represent no threat to skiers, but when buried by a fall of snow they immediately become a new layer of depth hoar and a potentially dangerous zone of weakness in the snowpack.

ARTIFICIAL SNOW

The discussion of hard, crusty surfaces leads naturally on to the vexed subject of artificial snow. For many years this approach to solving shortages of snow was seen in the Alps as a nasty North American habit, but the snow droughts of the late 1980s (*see* page 65) soon changed all that. Now snow-making is *de rigueur*, yet it still remains the subject of heated debate. Some of these issues relate to the wider environmental consequences of the overuse of local water supplies and the impact of longer lasting snow on the local ecology. For the purposes of this book, however, what matters is the type of snow produced – a subject of almost equal controversy.

The essential feature of snow-making is that it relies on freezing a plume of very fine water droplets that are sprayed into the air. This process will only work effectively if the temperature is well below freezing ($-3°C$ ($27°F$) or lower). So, in mild, dry weather ski resorts have no hope of improving conditions. This approach to making snow reproduces only part of the natural chain of events described in the previous section. Natural particles in the local water supplies or the addition of special harmless bacteria (*Pseudomonas syringae*), whose surface properties are particularly well suited to accelerate the freezing of the droplets, help to form a rain of fine ice crystals.

By their very nature, the crystals formed by the freezing of droplets already resemble the partially metamorphosed particles in natural snow. As a result, artificial snow, while providing a good substitute for piste skiing, tends to compact more readily and become hard and icy if not regularly manicured. Given that it is most frequently used to maintain heavily trafficked runs back to resorts, this is a small price to pay. What skiers have to remember is that as well as this snow being icy, it is often accompanied by an additional hazard: the absence of snow beside the runs. Skiers going too fast or out of control are therefore more likely to be injured if they career off the piste as there is no benign layer of snow to cushion their impact with the rocks and trees they encounter.

There is one other hazard with artificial snow, when it is used extensively to enhance the snow cover on all the runs, as in New England. The hard crust that is created presents a particular challenge to the piste-grooming machines, and sometimes they fail to break up the surface into a benevolent crystalline form, instead leaving paving slabs of rock-hard crust lurking in the piste. Known as 'death cookies', these slabs can bring your smooth progress to a juddering halt.

In spite of its limitations, artificial snow is now essential for a successful ski resort. Those low-level resorts, notably in Austria, that have refused to invest in snow-making equipment deserve no sympathy. If much higher resorts such as Alpe-d'Huez, Cervinia and Lech/Zürs can supplement their already substantial snowfall with extensive snow-making, the message is clear. It is therefore worth checking the ski guides (*see* Further Reading) and brochures to find out what the different resorts offer in this respect as even the emerging resorts of Chile are now taking the precaution of making snow.

Fig 2.8 *Air flowing over mountains is both lifted and squeezed. This produces heavier precipitation on the windward side and relatively dry conditions on the leeward side of the range. The wind-speed also increases towards the crest of the ridge and then decreases on the leeward side (see Fig 2.9).*

TOPOGRAPHY

So far it has been taken for granted that the higher we go the colder the air gets, but it is by no means obvious why this should be so. Moreover, the reason may be difficult to credit. It relates to the fact that when gas is forced to expand it has to do work to overcome the weak attraction between its component molecules. This is why the neck of a soda sparklet canister of CO_2 gets cold when the gas is released into the siphon. Conversely, compressing a gas causes it to heat up, which is why a bicycle pump gets hot when used to inflate tyres.

The lower 10–12km or so (33,000–39,000ft) of the atmosphere is continually being turned over by weather systems; where air rises it expands and cools, and where it sinks it is compressed and warms. This mixing process means that, on average, the temperature of the atmosphere falls by about 6.5°C for each kilometre (or 3.6°F every 1,000ft) in altitude. The decline in temperature with altitude is known as the **lapse rate** and can vary appreciably with weather conditions. When combined with the impact of the upland areas, the overall effect is for mountains to 'make their own weather'.

There are many variations in how mountains modify standard weather systems to produce increased snowfall and distribute it from place to place, but the simple model is not difficult to appreciate. As air is forced to rise over a range of mountains (*see* Fig 2.8), it cools and water vapour condenses to form clouds. Often these clouds may be additional to existing higher clouds that form part of wider weather systems. Whatever the situation, these clouds increase the amount of precipitation on the mountains, especially on the windward side of the range. In particular, if the upper clouds are producing precipitation, the additional lower-level clouds can enhance the precipitation process dramatically.

Another feature of this basic two-dimensional model is how the rising air is squeezed by the flow process, increasing the wind-speed over the crest of the range and then causing it to decline on the leeward side. When the model is extended to three dimensions, it is obvious these effects will occur in both the horizontal as well as the vertical plane. So, wind-speeds will increase as winds flow around the sides as well as over the top of the main features in a mountain range: they will be funnelled and accelerated over cols, and swirl and eddy down some valleys. The way the wind and clouds are swept up, around and through a mountain range produces all sorts of local effects, and it is these that lead to subtle variations both in the winds and in the distribution of snowfall.

Broadly speaking, in mid-latitudes the amount of precipitation increases by about a factor of two between sea-level and about 1,500m (5,000ft), and then by more than the same amount again around 3,000m (around 10,000ft). These figures are typical of the Alps and the Coast Ranges of North America. Further south the situation is more complicated. The western slopes of the Sierra Nevada tend to have a maximum precipitation at around 1,600m (5,250ft). Conversely, the western slopes of the Colorado Rockies show a much more rapid increase, with six times as much precipitation at around 3,200m (10,500ft) than in the foothills at around 1,750m (5,750ft). In Idaho, the amount of precipitation increases linearly with altitude more in tune with the Coast Ranges.

The level at which reliable snow cover occurs depends on a combination of temperature and precipitation. As a rule of thumb, locations where the average monthly temperature is below −3°C (27°F) will build up a snow base. Places that are slightly warmer but which have heavy precipitation, most of which falls as snow, will build up a base that can survive intermittent thaws. This can last well into spring as the mean temperature rises

above freezing. Conversely, dry areas may not maintain thin snow cover even though they experience lower temperatures. Of much greater importance, however, is where the snow collects, and this is all a matter of topography.

The basic model predicts that maximum precipitation will fall on the windward side of the mountain ranges. But, as will become clear in Chapters 4 and 5, the climatology of snowfall reflects a more complex interaction between prevailing weather patterns and the topography of the range. So, although much more snow falls on windward slopes in places such as British Columbia and Chile, where there are strong and persistent westerly winds, elsewhere the amount of snowfall requires more detailed analysis. Indeed, when we get down to local topography the reverse is often the case.

In the shelter of a ridge, the decline in wind-speed leads to more snow being deposited on the leeward side (see Fig 2.9). This build-up can produce increasingly dangerous conditions throughout the season and the associated risk of avalanches (see page 81). Where this build-up develops on sunny slopes, the combination of deep snow and frequent sunshine increases the chances of the snowpack becoming unstable. At the same time, shady combes in the lee of high ridges, such as Saulire at Courchevel, provide some of the most reliable skiing conditions, and safe examples of slopes such as this form an essential part of a successful resort's skiing armoury. Off-piste leeward slopes should, however, be treated with great caution, especially if the ridge exhibits evidence of forming a cornice of windblown snow and the slope catches the sun during the day.

On windward slopes the reverse is true. These often have their snow blown off, or, where they also catch the midday sun, the snow may be stripped away quickly. But

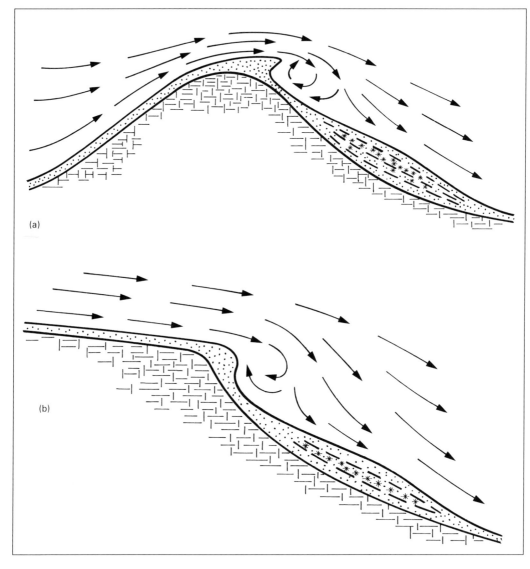

Fig 2.9 *How snow collects on leeward slopes. The cross-section of a ridge in (a) shows how snow cover on the windward side is thin, how a cornice forms at the ridge and how the wind deposits layers of deeper snow on the leeward side. These effects can also occur where there are changes in gradient (b); the formation of a cornice may then be the only sign of a dangerous build-up of snow lower down the slope.*

where the snow is deep enough to form a durable snowpack, it is liable to develop a hard wind-crust which is much less likely to avalanche.

3
Sun and Shade

So that the sun shall not burn thee by day:
neither the moon by night.
Book of Common Prayer 121:1

Sunshine is the other half of the equation for skiers, but, as with all such equations, getting the balance right is the difficult part. Most of our images of skiing are set in sun-drenched landscapes, but you can have too much of a good thing – for one thing, lengthy dry spells with unbroken sunshine by day can destroy the snow cover rapidly. In an ideal world it would snow every night and the sun would blaze down from a clear blue sky all day; in practice, however, the situation is often very different.

ASTRONOMICAL TRUTHS AND CLOUDINESS

The amount of sunshine experienced in the mountains is governed by the number of daylight hours and the frequency of cloud cover. The first is entirely predictable, while the second is anything but. However, with a knowledge of how the length of the day varies throughout the year, plus some climatological data about cloudiness, it is possible to form a reasonable view of where the chances of getting the best mix of snow and sun are greatest. This combination is best viewed in terms of both the length of the day and the height of the sun in the sky. Fig 3.1 shows how these factors vary between September and March in the northern hemisphere for three different latitudes, these spanning the most popular mountain areas. (For the southern hemisphere, all the dates have to be shifted by six months.)

The impact of day length is easy to appreciate: it defines the number of hours you can enjoy the mountains. The elevation of the sun, however, affects enjoyment in a variety of ways. When the sun is low in the sky its rays travel much further through the atmosphere. This not only reduces the amount of heat that reaches the ground but also alters the proportion of ultraviolet (UV) rays that cause sunburn (*see* page 24). If the sun is 30 degrees above the horizon, its rays pass through twice as much of the atmosphere than when it is directly overhead; when it sinks to 15 degrees it has nearly four times the atmospheric path to go through. Furthermore, at these oblique angles the beam is correspondingly spread out when it hits level ground. So, both the composition of the sunlight and its impact on the ground are profoundly altered when the sun is low in the sky.

As the curves in Fig 3.1 show, the further north you go the shorter the length of day. At 60°N (the latitude of the southern Norwegian resorts), the sun is above the horizon for only five hours and then only at the shallowest

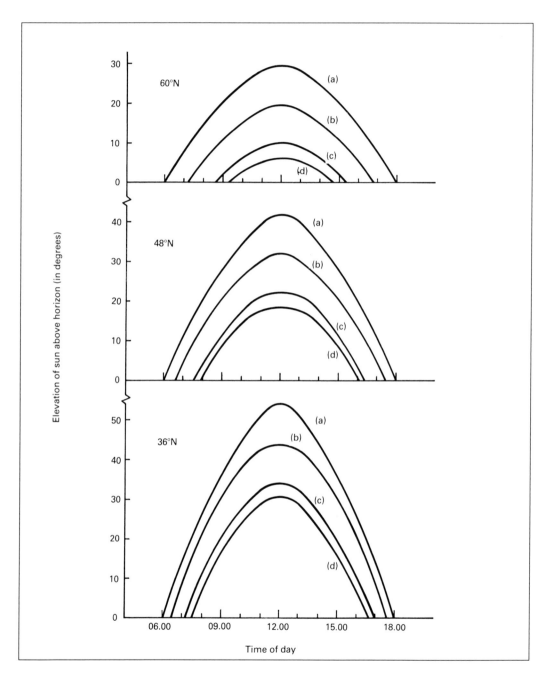

Fig 3.1   *The elevation of the sun above the horizon for three latitudes on: (a) 21 September and 21 March; (b) 21 October and 21 February; (c) 21 November and 21 January; and (d) 21 December.*

of angles during the winter solstice. By comparison, at 36°N (the latitude of the southernmost resorts in the Rockies), the same day is some nine hours long and the sun is more than 20 degrees above the horizon for five hours. The situation changes only slowly either side of the winter solstice, but beyond a month or so the days lengthen rapidly at high latitudes. By late February, the differences in the length of the day are small and cross over at the equinoxes. During the summer half of the year, the days are longer at high latitudes.

When it comes to the elevation of the sun, high latitudes are always at a disadvantage. During the central core of the two months on either side of the winter solstice, the sun never rises above 10 degrees in the sky at 60°N. Even by late February, the maximum elevation is still only 20 degrees, and it is not until after the spring equinox that it gets above 30 degrees. By comparison, the sun's elevation gets above 20 degrees in early January and above 30 degrees by mid-February in the Alps or northern Idaho and Montana (46°N to 48°N). So, the message is clear: the more northerly resorts, whatever their weather conditions, are a bad bet for sunshine in December and January. Moreover, if resorts in these regions are usually cloudy then this, combined with the low angle of the sun, makes for unremittingly gloomy conditions. Thereafter, as the days lengthen the low elevation of the sun can be a benefit, for not only does it mean that the snow may last longer, but it also reduces the risk of sunburn. Before considering these factors, however, we need first to discuss the absorption and reflection properties of snow and its surroundings.

REFLECTION AND ABSORPTION

Even in mountain areas where the combination of reliable snow and frequent sunshine provides a good chance of excellent skiing, the combination of reflection and absorption of sunlight can produce a wide variety of conditions. The central factor to consider is the high reflectivity of snow. New snow can reflect over 80 per cent of incident solar energy back into space. As the snow ages this drops to around 50 per cent, but even so the figure is far higher than that of other surfaces – typically, bare rock, exposed pasture or trees without snow cover will absorb between 80 and 90 per cent of the sunlight falling on them. This means that the amount and extent of snow, together with its age, can have a profound effect on the local temperature conditions.

Shade Temperature

Before discussing the effects on snow of temperature, we need to address one of the most basic, but also one of the most widely misunderstood features of meteorology – the shade temperature. All reliable temperature measurements are made under standard conditions, obtained by positioning instruments in a well-ventilated screened white box (called a Stevenson Shelter) that is at a set height of 4ft (1.146m) above ground level and preferably located above a standard grassy surface away from trees. The reason for being so specific about this is the fact that the shade air temperature is the most meaningful measure of weather conditions. Where the readings are affected either directly when the thermometer absorbs sunlight or indirectly when heat is absorbed by dark surfaces around the measurement site or by radiation reflected from the ground on to the thermometer, they will tell you more about the properties of the thermometer or its surroundings than the actual air temperature.

This may seem like pedantry, as the temperature in the sun often seems so much more important. I have sat on the balcony of a restaurant at 2,560m (8,400ft) above Val d'Isère in shirt sleeves in the bright December sunshine feeling pleasantly warm. Behind me a digital thermometer proclaimed that the temperature was 26°C (79°F), but the snow on the adjacent slopes in the sun was not melting and in the shade it remained crisp and powdery. Moreover, if cloud had obscured the sun or a stiff breeze had sprung up, both the recorded temperature and that felt by me would have plummeted to below freezing.

This explains why in the tables in the Appendix, places such as Säntis show a day-time temperature that normally does not rise above 0°C (32°F) during January and February, in spite of the fact that on bright, calm, sunny days the conditions will feel pleasantly warm in the sun. The shade temperature is therefore what matters in terms of understanding the local climate and the average conditions that will be found at any given site. The effects of sun and shade are, however, central to the distribution and durability of snow cover, as well as to the comfort of anyone enjoying the mountains in winter.

Melting Snow

The high absorption coefficients of surfaces other than snow mean that the durability of snow cover depends on both its depth and uniformity, as well as the amount of sunshine falling on it. Wherever the underlying surface shows through the snow, the surface will warm up rapidly in bright sunshine, the rate of this depending on how high the sun is in the sky and the aspect of the slopes. Exposed

south-facing slopes in spring are most vulnerable, and the moment breaks appear in the snow cover rapid melting will occur – even when the air temperature is well below freezing. The snow lasts much better where the sun strikes the ground at a more oblique angle or when there is shade for part of the day. In March and April better conditions are found on north-facing slopes and also down among the trees where, in spite of higher temperatures, shade protects the snow.

Even where the depth of snow is adequate, the sun can alter its properties. When the air temperature rises to approach freezing, the amount of heat absorbed by the surface of the snow is sufficient to produce melting. If this process goes too far it can be a confounded nuisance, producing heavy slush which then freezes into rock-hard ruts when the sun goes down. However, before this stage is reached the melting process can produce one of the miracles of skiing – spring snow conditions. This is the short period between ice and slush when a microscopically thin layer of water forms on the surface grains of snow to provide perfect lubrication for the skis. When this occurs it is possible to glide over the snow effortlessly but with maximum control – an exhilarating combination.

Because of the subtle way in which the sun, snow and air temperature affect the timing of these conditions, it is possible to find spring snow throughout the day later in the season in a large resort; the trick is to know where to go. The safest method is to use a guide whose fund of local knowledge will allow him or her to pinpoint the best spots. If you are on your own, however, the obvious place to start is on the lower, sunny slopes in the morning and transfer gradually to higher, shaded runs as the snow softens up. The timing of this trek may take several days to master and can easily be confused by varying weather conditions. Better results may be achieved by finding west-facing, tree-lined runs where the combination of aspect and trees means that first the sunny side and then the initially shaded areas undergo the transition gradually as the day goes by. Whichever approach is adopted, the planning is well worth the effort as it enables you to use a little physical insight to get far more out of the available conditions.

The benefits of thinking ahead also apply at the end of the day. Since runs back to the resort can become very busy, it often pays to avoid the most heavily used routes and take what is ostensibly a more difficult way back. A quiet red or even black run down through the trees may be easier than a green or blue run which has been in the sun for much of the day – the green run back into la Daille at Val d'Isère is a good example, as are runs back into les Deux Alpes, Méribel and Saas-Fee. As the sun goes down on such heavily used runs, soft snow freezes and combines with the expanses of ocean-blue ice which build up during the season to produce a sloping skating rink. To these basic ingredients are added the spice of exposed rocks, and the many beginners or modest skiers who lie spreadeagle on the piste or perch quaking on top of the only decent spots to execute a turn. This obstacle course is a trial to good skiers and a nightmare for the less competent. Rather than spoil an otherwise good day out, the brave should therefore use ostensibly more difficult runs, while the cautious should feel no shame in taking a lift down to the bottom.

SHELTER FROM THE STORM

Skiing among the trees also offers shelter from adverse weather, which can combine poor visibility, biting winds and very low temperatures. Above the tree-line any one of these conditions can make skiing difficult, but when they occur together it can be unbearable. On runs among the trees, however, it is much easier to stay on course in bad visibility as the trees themselves provide a frame of reference as well as acting as a windbreak. In the case of low temperatures, it is more a case of looking for both shelter from any wind and finding the least cold conditions. When intense cold spells, such as those of January 1987 and February 1991, engulf high resorts in the Alps such as Cervinia, Obergurgl, Tignes or Val Thorens, which have little skiing among the trees, there is no hiding place. At times like these, the enviable snow records of the resorts is no consolation, for all skiers want are low, sheltered spots where they can enjoy the excellent snow in some degree of comfort. Shelter is particularly valuable for beginners and children who may not have become converted to the attractions of skiing; going to a resort where lessons in the bitter cold are the only option may frighten them off for life.

In the western United States and Canada, where bitingly cold spells are more common, the benefit of the trees is essential. The higher tree-line does, however, mean that more than half the skiing is amongst the trees in most of these resorts. The exceptions are resorts such as Arapahoe Basin in Colorado, Grand Targhee in Wyoming and Big Sky in Montana, which have more skiing at higher levels than their neighbours. Even in well-wooded resorts, however, the occasional intense cold is one of the most common complaints of visitors from Europe.

Visibility

Loss of visibility is difficult to describe and photographs fail to convey the sudden changes that can occur on the mountains. This is because many of the changes that

23

really matter involve tiny changes in contrast. In brilliant sunshine the smallest undulations and variations in the snow cover stand out clearly, casting shadows or reflecting different amounts of sunlight. As the light diminishes under even moderate cloud cover, the shadows disappear and the snow becomes a uniform white. Long before you are enveloped in thick cloud, both skiing and navigating in this featureless landscape can be a challenge, with even gradual slopes becoming difficult to interpret. In such conditions, skiers should stick to well-marked pistes. For hillwalkers, a good knowledge of the planned route, accurate maps and the ability to navigate precisely using a compass are the essential components for safely negotiating the way in deteriorating visibility.

It is not possible to give precise figures for how visibility drops off in cloud. With puffy cumulus clouds that spread up the valley, the visibility may drop as low as 10m (30ft). Oddly enough, in older clouds that are precipitating, the visibility may be much greater even though they may look much more threatening than their puffy cousins. The reason for this is that once there are appreciable numbers of snowflakes and sizeable water droplets, the process of evaporation and vapour transport quickly mops up the tiniest droplets. It is these tiny droplets which play a major part in reducing visibility and which are present in vast numbers (hundreds of millions per cubic metre) in newly formed thick cloud.

ULTRAVIOLET RADIATION AND SUNBURN

What with the hole in the ozone layer and increased incidence of skin cancer, ultraviolet (UV) radiation has been much in the news in recent years. Because ozone screens out most of the damaging UV rays that cause sunburn and skin cancer, there has been growing concern about the risks of sunbathing. The fact that bright sunshine is an essential ingredient of a successful skiing holiday and plays an important part in enjoying other mountain activities means that we need to know more about the risk of exposure to the sun when at high altitudes.

Of the solar radiation hitting the top of the atmosphere, some 39 per cent falls in the visible region (wavelengths of 400–780nm), 56 per cent falls in the infra-red region (wavelengths longer than 780nm), and just 5 per cent in the ultraviolet (UV) region (wavelengths shorter than 400nm).

Ultraviolet rays are defined in terms of their capacity to damage the skin. UV rays of longer wavelengths (320–400nm), which make up 98 per cent of all the UV, are defined as UVA and do relatively little damage to the skin. The remaining 2 per cent of UV rays have wavelengths of 290–320nm (the tiny amounts of radiation at wavelengths below 290nm are absorbed by oxygen high in the atmosphere and are of no concern here). These short-wavelength UV rays are known as UVB and are strongly absorbed by the skin, where they cause inflammation and are capable of damaging DNA (the genetic material in our body cells). The skin is between a hundred and a thousand times more sensitive to UVB than UVA. It is therefore UVB, which is partially absorbed by ozone in the stratosphere, that is the principal target for sun lotions used to protect the skin.

The tiny quantities of ozone in the lower atmosphere, together with dust and aerosols, absorb some of the UVB in sunlight. Therefore, the higher you go in the mountains, the less the UVB absorption and the stronger the UVB 'dose'. Roughly speaking, the sunburning power increases by 4 per cent with every 300m (1,000ft) in altitude. At an altitude of

3,000m (10,000ft) you will receive about 50 per cent more UVB on average in the direct rays of the sun than you would at sea-level for the same solar elevation in the sky. When the sun is more than 30 degrees above the horizon (*see* Fig 3.1), the risk of severe sunburn at high altitudes is therefore considerable.

If the high reflectivity of the snow is also taken into account, it can be calculated that in late March at noon in, say, Aspen at an altitude of 3,000m (10,000ft), exposed skin is likely to receive roughly twice as much UVB as it would on a Mediterranean beach in high summer. Even at the higher latitude of Val d'Isère, the exposure would be around a half to three-quarters as much again as the sea-level summer value. Clearly, such intense exposure will soon cause severe sunburn if no preventative action is taken. It is also important to remember that thin or moderate cloud still lets a lot of UVB through: complete light cloud cover allows about half of the UVB through. It is therefore vital to take preventative action in all but the thickest cloud cover conditions once the sun is high in the sky.

In considering prevention, this book will stick to the problems of UVB and sunburn. Although the issues of skin cancer and ageing are important, in terms of holidays in the mountains it is the immediate consequence of sunburn that can spoil your fun. The continuing medical debate of the possible damage caused by UVA will also be left on one side, but, that said, it is wise to use a sunscreen that provides UVA as well as UVB protection (UVA protection is indicated by stars, with more stars showing a greater degree of protection).

There is, however, one aspect of these long-term effects that cannot be ignored, and that is that sunburn in childhood can significantly increase the risk of developing skin cancer later in life. The advice that follows is therefore even more important for children, but, at any age, painful and disfiguring sunburn not only ruins a holiday but is a sign of potential long-term damage to the skin.

Protecting Against Sunburn

What really matters is avoiding exposure to too much UVB. Recent measurements showing that there has been a decline in stratospheric ozone do not alter the basic message, but simply reinforce the importance of taking care. There are three ways of avoiding sunburn: stay out of the sun, especially around noon; wear adequate clothing; and anoint exposed skin with sun cream. The first is not a serious option when climbing, skiing or walking. The second is basically a question of what to wear in order to protect your head, face and neck.

First and foremost, you must wear goggles or sun-glasses. Most types will do as both glass and plastic screen out UVB effectively, but it is wise to choose products that claim to do the job well or take the advice of your optician. The alternative is to run a real risk of snow blindness (*ophthalmia nivialis*), which is basically sunburn of the surface of the cornea. While this is usually only a temporary phenomenon, it is excruciatingly painful and totally incapacitates the sufferer for several days – not the ideal combination for an enjoyable holiday. So, don't worry about developing 'panda eyes'; they are a rite of passage. Sunbathing with your eyes closed is also not a good idea as you may burn your eyelids. A wide-brimmed hat can also help, providing you can manage to ski with it on, but it is not completely effective as it offers little protection when the sun is at a relatively low angle and none from UVB reflected up off the snow.

The third method of avoiding sunburn is the one most widely adopted. Effective sun lotions contain organic compounds which absorb UVB very strongly and cut out quite a lot of UVA. Laboratory tests using, of all things, hairless mouse epidermis, have shown that the lotions do perform well. As a rule, the protection factor number indicates how much longer you can stay in the sun before burning than when unprotected: factor 2 enables you to double your exposure time, factor 4 quadruples it, and so on. But in real life things are more complicated. Not only is it difficult to apply the product uniformly, but wind, relative humidity and perspiration can all alter the amount of protection significantly. So, err on the side of caution, and apply liberal quantities of high-factor sun block at the start of the holiday and reapply this every two hours while out in the sun. As noted earlier, this regular application is of even more importance for children.

If you start to build up a tan, then you can ease back a bit if you wish to have something to show for your efforts. But remember, even the strongest sun block allows some UVB to get through, so any changes in application should be gradual as it becomes clear whether or not you are catching the sun with the current regimen. In effect, what you will be doing is maintaining a balancing act between the artificial sun screen you are applying and any natural protection in the form of melanin in the skin.

This personal assessment leads back to the most fundamental fact about sunburn: what type of skin you have. If you are among the 15–20 per cent of Europeans who burn easily and tan minimally or not at all then you should stick to the maximum sun block and not be tempted to ease off during the holiday. If you are in the majority, who burn moderately and tan gradually, then the incremental approach can be adopted to reflect your personal position. The remaining 15–20 per cent, who burn rarely and tan profusely, can adopt a more relaxed approach after some acclimatization to the fiercer conditions at altitude. As a general rule, however, it is much better to use too much rather than too little sunscreen, whatever your skin type. Do not worry about the tan, for even with such precautions you will still look disgustingly healthy to your whey-faced colleagues when you return to work.

4

Weather Systems and Patterns

Omnia mutantor, et nos mutanter in illis.
(All things change, and we change with them.)
Emperor Lothar I (795–855)

The Earth's atmosphere is a thin shell encapsulating the planet, with half its mass lying below an altitude of 5km (16,400ft). The major mountain ranges project up to and beyond this level, so they have a major impact on the weather systems that swirl continually around the globe and on the paths they follow. There is insufficient space in this book to go into much of the detail of the meteorology of global weather (*see* Further Reading if you would like more information), but instead we will concentrate on how mountain ranges alter the behaviour of standard weather systems. The emphasis will be placed on the middle latitudes, not only because the most frequently visited mountains lie in these regions, but also because it is here, in the winter half of the year, that the most dynamic weather systems are to be found.

DEPRESSIONS

Low-pressure systems (depressions) are the real movers and shakers in winter weather. Even in the depths of polar winter at high latitudes, the Earth radiates a lot of energy into space, at the same time receiving virtually none from the sun. As a result, huge amounts of energy must be transported from the Equator to the poles via ocean currents and in the atmosphere, this reaching a peak in winter. Since ocean currents remain roughly constant throughout the year, the additional energy must be carried polewards in winter by increasingly intense and frequent mid-latitude depressions.

If we were to combine all the weather-satellite images taken during any January to produce a movie of the weather patterns as viewed from the North Pole, we would see a continuous circumpolar vortex. A steady stream of circular eddies of clouds moving east and north would be seen heading for the Arctic. Closer inspection of this maelstrom would show that, like a flow of shallow water over shoals and projecting rocks, the patterns were related to the distribution of the mountains in the northern hemisphere. So, the most important depression tracks would be seen over the Pacific and Atlantic, but as they approached the continents, their course would be influenced and altered by the mountain ranges. Skirting the highest land and picking energy from inland seas such as the

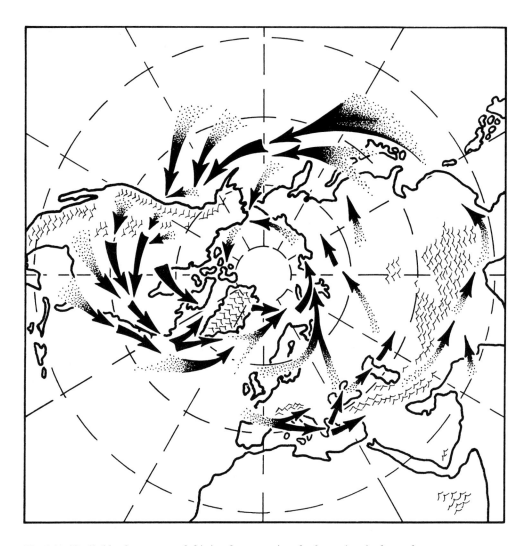

Fig 4.1 *Fuelled by the oceans and skirting the mountains, the depressions in the northern hemisphere in January flow continually polewards. This diagram shows the principal tracks as solid arrows, with the arrowheads indicating areas where the depressions are most likely to be found. The stippled tracks depict regions of less frequent low-pressure activity.*

Mediterranean and Black Sea, the depression tracks would form a hemispherical merry-go-round. Furthermore, in successive years the preferred tracks might alter significantly.

Long-term statistics show that the principal depression tracks run across the North Pacific towards the Gulf of Alaska and also towards Vancouver Island (*see* Fig 4.1). The northerly track is then diverted southwards and combines with the more southerly track to run across North America at a latitude of around 50°N. At the same time, this interaction with the mountains of Canada and the northern United States tends to generate eddies to the east of the Sierra Nevada. These tracks are then reinforced as they cross the Rockies to form a major track across the Midwest. In addition, depressions spawned in the Gulf of Mexico run up the east coast and join with the other systems crossing North America to stimulate reinvigorated depressions running across the North Atlantic.

The principal track across the North Atlantic is up towards Iceland, with branches running up either side of Greenland. This pattern creates a semi-permanent low (the 'Icelandic low') which covers much of the area between the British Isles and Greenland, and serves to slough off secondary depressions which most frequently run across Scotland and into the Baltic. Other secondary depressions dive out of the Bay of Biscay between the Pyrenees and the Alps into the Mediterranean basin. Here, the warm water revitalizes them and they follow major tracks up into the Black Sea, along the southern coast of Turkey and into the Middle East. Further east, the tracks are less well defined and their position is controlled by the Himalayas.

If viewed throughout the winter, this circumpolar vortex would be seen to expand until January and then contract again as spring is approached. This expansion towards lower latitudes and back again triggers the more southerly tracks, the result being that precipitation in such places – for example, California – is almost wholly concentrated in the winter half of the year (see Table A.5). When different years are compared, this pattern is, however, less easy to see as the tracks may deviate substantially for weeks, or even months on end. Moreover, there are considerable variations in the frequency and intensity of the depressions. All of these variations define the fluctuations in winter weather from year to year (see page 35).

The overall picture of winter circulation in the northern hemisphere indicates that the relatively warm oceans are the breeding grounds for depressions. The major mountain ranges do, however, play an important role in the paths the depressions follow and how they both dissipate their energy and then pick up steam again. This broad conclusion is reinforced by the circulation pattern in the southern hemisphere, where the tracks are much simpler and are concentrated in the latitude band 35°S to 55°S during the austral winter.

Depression Characteristics

At the detailed level, each depression has a distinct life cycle lasting three to five days. The central feature of the model is the separation of two masses whose temperature is different and whose boundary is normally sharp. Along the fronts, which mark this boundary, temperature and wind direction change suddenly, and in most cases the state of the sky alters likewise. Sections of the front are named according to their motion: a warm front is the boundary along which warm air displaces cold air; a cold front has the reverse characteristics. The cross-section of a typical depression (see Fig 4.2) shows wedges of cold air under warm air to the south of its centre. To the north of its centre, the cold front forms a trough filled with warm air. The overall effect is to raise warm air, thereby creating extensive layers of cloud and precipitation in the region of the warm and cold fronts. To balance this lifting process, cold air descends to fill the void created by the rising warm air.

The Effect of Mountains

While the standard model of first deepening and then stagnating depressions is a familiar

29

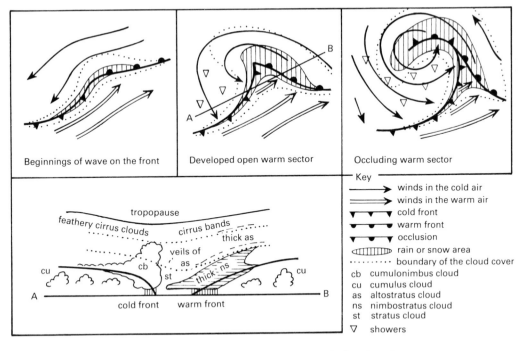

Fig. 4.2 Three stages in the development of a frontal cyclone and vertical section along the line AB. Invert the maps for the southern hemisphere. (Source: Climate: Past, Present and Future Vol I, Methuen, 1972.)

feature of daily weather maps in the newspapers and on television, the associated vertical motions are less well known, but they do play an essential part in how mountains create their own weather. Where air is rising, as in the warm sector of a depression, the uplift generated by running into a mountain range (see Fig 2.8) accentuates the precipitation process. Where air is descending, as behind a cold front, collision with mountains can slow progress: the front can get wrapped around the range and produce much longer periods of precipitation than before or after the encounter. This, in part, explains why a cold front sweeping across France that is associated with a deep depression over of the British Isles (see Fig 4.3) can produce far heavier snowfall around the Mont Blanc mas-

sif and down to the Tarentaise than elsewhere in the Alps. Once such fronts have cleared the obstruction, they often accelerate effectively to catch up with the rest of the weather system, so leaving very little snow on the leeward side of the range.

A strong westerly flow associated with storm tracks closer to the Alps can have a more dramatic interaction with the mountains, whereby eddies in the lee are generated which trigger the formation of a new low-pressure system. This process, known as **cyclogenesis**, is most common in the lee of the Front Range in Colorado, to the south of the Rockies over Arizona and New Mexico, and in the Gulf of Genoa just below the Alps, and explains the strong tracks that originate in these regions (see Fig 4.1). These new sys-

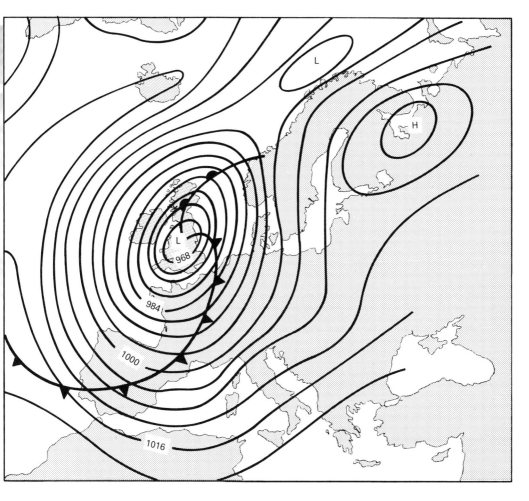

Fig 4.3 *Heavy snow heading towards the Alps. An example (29 January 1978) of the type of deep depression that can bring unsettled weather to the Alps. Not only did the cold front advancing across France foreshadow heavy snow, but it triggered an additional low-pressure system in the lee of the Alps which prolonged the snowfall.*

tems can deepen rapidly and produce heavy snowfall on the adjacent mountains, thus partially counterbalancing the rain shadow effect on the leeward side of the Rockies and the Alps. In particular, the process contributes to the heavier snowfall over the San Juan Mountains.

In extreme circumstances, cyclogenesis can result in a secondary area of low pressure effectively loitering around the Alps for days on end as successive fronts pile in from the Atlantic. The situation shown in Fig 4.3 was part of just such a stormy period which lasted for nearly two weeks. It led to extreme avalanche conditions in the French Alps, Switzerland and the Val d'Aosta resorts (notably Cervinia), and my two-week family holiday in Avoriaz was largely snowed off as even the nursery slopes were shut for days on end because the snow was so deep and dangerous. This was clearly a case of bad timing on my part, because the subsequent two weeks had combined settled weather with brilliant snow conditions.

ANTICYCLONES

In comparison to depressions, anticyclones are relatively lethargic beasts, but this does not stop them playing an equal part in defining conditions in the mountains. For, although anticyclones are passive and pushed around by low-pressure systems for much of the time, they are capable of taking root with great obstinacy. When this happens they control the weather for long periods. Even in their mobile form anticyclones can bring invigorating interludes of clear, colder weather between successive depressions, often providing the only opportunities for good skiing during stormy winters. As such, anticyclones are little more than ridges that glide along the border of the much larger semi-permanent high-pressure areas in the subtropics, but it is their more static form that is of greater interest. Known as 'blocking' anticyclones, because they interrupt the normal westerly flow of depressions in mid-latitudes, these static systems can be a dominant feature in winter weather.

European Anticyclones

Anticyclones are areas of descending air and hence their interaction with mountains is less dramatic than is the case with depressions. Over Europe there are two principal forms of long-lived high-pressure systems that exert a major influence on the Alps and the Pyrenees. The first occurs when low-pressure systems run continually up across Iceland and the subtropical anticyclone that normally lurks down around the Azores extends up across Europe and the Mediterranean (*see* Fig 4.4). This brings very mild conditions to the British Isles and calm, often foggy weather to the lowlands around the Alps. However, at higher levels it brings unbroken sunshine by day and frost by night. In the short term this provides blissful skiing conditions (providing there is already an adequate base), but, if it lasts for more than two months with no appreciable break, as it did in early 1989, the daytime snowmelt is not replenished by new fall.

The other form of long-lived anticyclone is a separate static system at higher latitudes. Often this is an extension of the permanent winter high-pressure system over Siberia, which forms a separate cell over Scandinavia or the British Isles (*see* Fig 4.5). It results in bitterly cold weather over Europe, with the depressions diverted up into the Arctic or down into the Mediterranean. Depending on the precise position of the system, the Alps and the Pyrenees will either be engulfed in intensely cold air (as happened in January 1987 and February 1991), or catch the fringes of the storms running through the Mediterranean. Alternatively, this type of anticyclone can develop over the North Atlantic and then form a bubble that drifts slowly eastwards and takes up residence over northern Europe. This brings similar but slightly less cold conditions.

If a blocking pattern sits over Europe for much of the winter, the southern side of the Alps tends to get more snow, while cold, dry conditions prevail on the northern slopes. In particular, low-pressure systems over Italy (*see* Fig 4.5) often bring heavy snow to the Dolomites and the southern Tyrol. This means that during the coldest winters in northern Europe, the best skiing conditions may well be found in the Italian resorts.

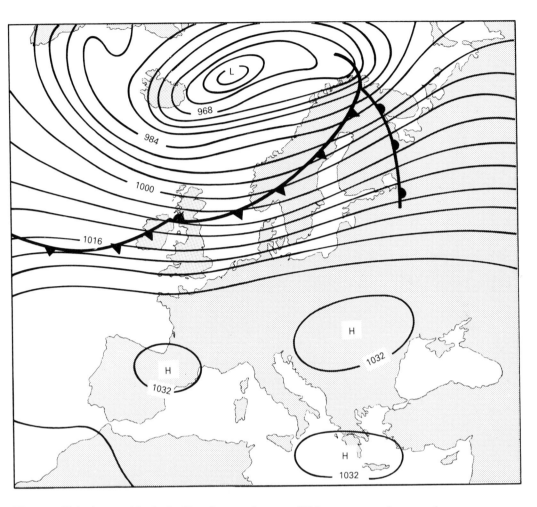

Fig 4.4 *Unbroken sunshine in the Alps. An extensive area of high pressure covering most of Europe (4 February 1989) brings clear skies to the mountains and fog in the valleys; the nearest precipitation is over northern England.*

North American Anticyclones

In North America similar patterns occur, although they do take a somewhat different form. The standard blocking conditions occur when high pressure develops off the west coast of the continent. This pushes milder air and depressions further north into Alaska. At the same time, surges of high pressure sweep arctic air down across the eastern half of the United States. As a result, the Coast Ranges suffer a shortage of snow, while the east coast mountains experience a mixture of heavy snow interspersed with cold waves of great ferocity. In the middle, the Rockies, which play a pivotal role in these weather patterns (*see* page 35), may get neither one thing nor the other.

The other situation which alters the run of depressions from the Gulf of Alaska into the

33

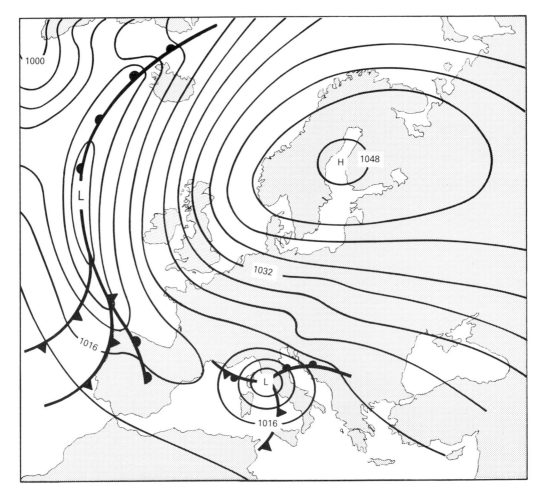

Fig 4.5 *Siberian winds sweep across northern Europe. An intense blocking anticyclone over the Gulf of Bothnia (6 February 1991) brings intense cold to the Alps and regions further north, while low-pressure systems either run up into the Arctic or down into the Mediterranean basin.*

continent is when the semi-permanent high pressure over the Yukon expands and builds up to a central pressure in excess of about 1,050mb. The influence of this dense mass of intensely cold air extends over the Coast Ranges, even though at low levels the coldest air is held back by the mountains. The arrival of brilliant clear conditions makes a dramatic change to the cloudy and stormy weather that is the norm for the Coast Ranges (*see* page 51).

Southern Hemisphere Anticyclones

In the mid-latitudes of the southern hemisphere, the absence of major continental land masses means that the zonal circulation is stronger and the influence of static high-pressure systems correspondingly weaker. As a consequence, the mountains of Chile and the South Island of New Zealand are subjected to the more steady stream of depressions that are such a feature of the roaring forties and screaming fifties. However, even here there are fluctuations throughout the winter and from year to year.

GLOBAL WEATHER PATTERNS

The description of depressions and anticyclones so far gives the impression that the weather patterns associated with them are largely predictable. However, as we all know the movement of these weather systems beyond a day or two seems anything but predictable in reality. The key to understanding these longer term changes lies in knowing what controls the broader weather patterns which determine the tracks and intensity of depressions. If we knew why the weather settled down into one pattern for several days or weeks before switching to another prolonged spell, then we would have the basis for the types of forecast that could be used for long-term activity planning. In truth, however, meteorologists have not cracked this problem (see page 67), so what we have to do is describe the symptoms of how the weather gets stuck in a rut and then consider whether the chances of it staying put for a week or more is high. While this falls a long way short of true long-term forecasting, it can still be useful for planning the details of a holiday in the mountains. It therefore helps to know a little more about these patterns.

The Jet Stream

The fundamental feature of global weather patterns in mid-latitudes is the existence of long waves in the atmosphere above an altitude of about 3km (10,000ft). The wavelength of these is measured in thousands of kilometres and the waves themselves generally migrate from west to east. The waves are superimposed on a strong zonal current, the core of which is known as the jet stream. The places where the jet stream is strongest in winter reflect the distribution of the oceans and the continents in the northern hemisphere. The important factor is the strong temperature gradients that exist at low levels in the atmosphere between the cold continents and the relatively warm oceans. The winter jet stream is therefore strongest near the east coast of Asia, over the eastern United States and over North Africa.

The importance of the jet stream is that it tends to steer the paths of the depressions. So, while the average picture is as described earlier in this chapter, shifts in the wavelength of the upper-atmosphere winds can lead to completely different patterns and spells of abnormal weather. The essential change is a switch between a strong longwave pattern and a meandering short-wave pattern. The former is associated with strong westerly winds at low level that sweep depressions along the standard tracks, while the latter is characterized by the blocking anticyclones described on page 32. These blocking anticyclones appear to be an essential feature of the atmospheric circulation in the northern hemisphere, where they limit the build-up of westerly winds by splitting the airflow into two streams that run north and south of the block. Most frequently they occur close to the Greenwich meridian and over the eastern Pacific. Normally they last up to two weeks, but they can persist much longer. They are more common in the Pacific, but in both principal locations they are usually a feature of the climate for between forty and sixty days a year.

The cause of blocking anticyclones is still

the subject of scientific debate. The distribution of the continents, mountains and oceans in the northern hemisphere plays a crucial role in their location, this idea being reinforced by the fact that blocking is much less common in the southern hemisphere, tending only to occur to the south and east of Australia and New Zealand. Computer models suggest that the heating effect of Australia is the dominant factor in this process, while, somewhat surprisingly, the Andes seem to exert less influence. These results are at odds with earlier computer modelling work which concluded that the links between the jet stream and the mountain ranges in the northern hemisphere offered the key to long-range forecasts. At a certain critical combination of speed and direction, an exaggerated standing wave could build up between the Himalayas and the Rockies, producing ideal conditions for blocking over the eastern Pacific. However, events in the 1980s contradicted this conclusion and indicated that periods of abnormal weather in the tropics are more important influencing factors (*see* page 67).

INTERACTIONS WITH THE MOUNTAINS

Turning to the detailed aspects of how weather systems combine with mountain ranges to produce the weather we experience, we have to get into the realms of physics. However, to get to grips with why the conditions vary so much from place to place, and go beyond the broad principles described in Chapter 2 and in the preceding sections of this chapter, we must delve a little deeper. In particular, there are two aspects of the interaction that deserve more attention: the first examines how weather systems are modified by mountains and what this leads to in terms of distribution of conditions across any

given range; while the second covers the specific examples of föhn winds in the Alps and chinook winds in western North America.

Lapse Rates

Clearly, mountains present a barrier to weather systems, forcing air to rise as it passes over them. In Chapter 2 the term lapse rate was introduced and the figure of a 6.5°C drop in temperature per kilometre gained in altitude (3.6°F per 1,000ft) was given. In practice, the figure for any particular parcel of rising air depends on whether or not condensation is taking place. As water vapour condenses, it releases heat and so reduces the rate of cooling with increased altitude – hence, the rate of cooling depends on how much moisture is in the air. Humid tropical air, once it starts to condense, will only cool at about 3.5°C per kilometre (1.9°F per 1,000ft). In temperate latitudes, the lapse rate of low-level clouds is typically around 5°C per kilometre (2.7°F per 1,000ft), whereas at levels where the temperature is below freezing it rises to around 7°C per kilometre (3.8°F per 1,000ft). Where there is no condensation, rising air cools at a constant rate of 10°C per kilometre (5.4°F per 1,000ft).

To distinguish between the differing behaviour patterns of rising air, meteorologists attach labels to the two processes: the cooling associated with condensation is known as the **saturated adiabatic lapse rate** (SALR); in the case of dry air, it is defined as the **dry adiabatic lapse rate** (DALR). However, where there is turbulent mixing, or rising and sinking air, the observed lapse rate will have an intermediate value. More complicated weather systems can exhibit exotic lapse rates which reflect air movements and surface heating and cooling effects over time, including warming with increased altitude at some levels.

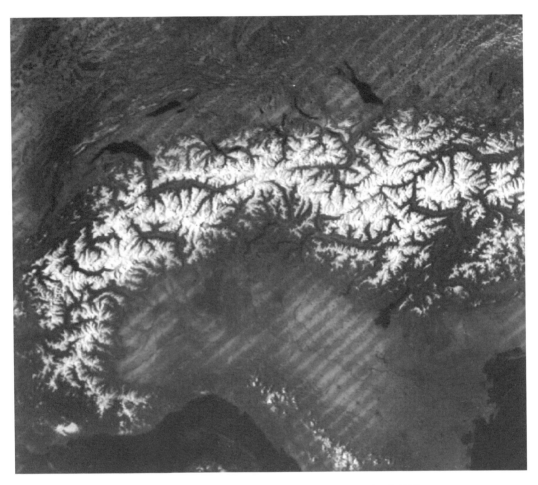

Fig 4.6   *The Alps as seen from space. A weather-satellite image taken on 17 April 1987 at 13.31 hours, which shows the complicated structure of the mountain range. (Reproduced with permission of the University of Dundee.)*

Effects of Topography

As well as forcing moving air to rise, often leading to condensation, mountains also alter the wind fields associated with weather systems by compressing and accelerating air as it passes over the crests of the range. On the leeward side, the winds will decrease and often form wave-like patterns (*see* Fig 2.8). At the same time, air funnelled through gaps in the peaks will accelerate and then slow down. These changes, together with the associated temperature variations, govern the weather in the mountains.

Diagrams such as Fig 2.8 provide a simplified picture of what is going on. In the real world, the complicated nature of any mountain range produces a wide variety of conditions over a short distance. Viewed from space, the true nature of the major ranges (*see*

37

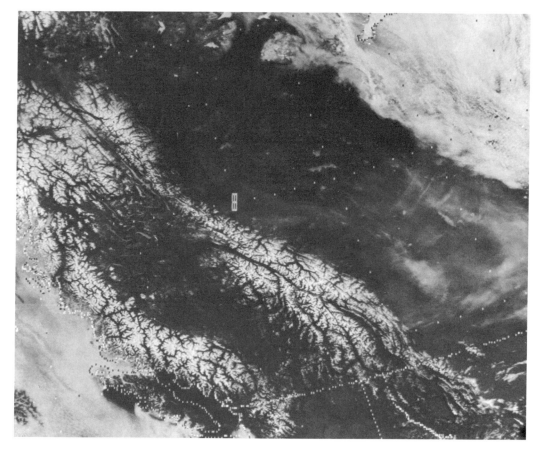

Fig 4.7   *The mountains of western Canada as seen from space. A weather-satellite image taken on 21 April 1991 showing the complicated structure of both the Coast Ranges and the Rockies. (Reproduced with permission of the US National Oceanic & Atmospheric Administration.)*

Figs 4.6 and 4.7) is clear to see. The Alps look like a great crumpled banana, dissected by deep valleys which cut into the range at many different angles. So, depending on the direction in which weather systems approach, at any given spot the impact of the mountains can be radically different. This means that it is not possible to predict precisely how the weather will vary from place to place. But, as we will see in Chapter 5, distinct patterns are discernible over the year, and there are a number of relatively simple processes that contribute to these variations.

The starting point for exploring these differences in more detail may seem somewhat surprising, and lies in the development of global computer models for weather forecasting. In the early 1980s the European Centre for Medium Range Weather Forecasting (ECMWF) discovered a technique for dealing with the tricky problem of representing mountains in their global weather models.

Because the horizontal separation of grid points in their models at that time was of the order of 100km (62 miles), ranges such as the Alps and the Rockies were covered by relatively few points. If the average elevation used for each 100km (62-mile) square was represented by a single grid point, then these mighty mountain ranges were smoothed out into far from impressive plateaux.

To reflect the real world where air is forced to skirt the highest peaks, a more realistic representation had to be developed. The result was to increase the height of the grid points to represent a combination of peaks and valleys filled with stagnant air. Called **envelope orography**, the technique improved the performance of medium-range weather forecasts (five to seven days ahead) by more than half a day. This provides useful insights into how mountains trap air and alter the weather locally, and also helps to explain why some resorts are better protected from sudden changes in the weather patterns. In the short term, these fluctuations effectively pass over the heads of those resorts hidden away deep within the mountain ranges. In the Alps, shelter from mild southerly or southwesterly winds by a pocket of cold, stagnant air may delay the onset of a damaging thaw by a day or two. This can make a considerable difference over the course of a typically variable winter, as the cumulative effect on the snowpack builds up over the season.

The Föhn and the Chinook

When not squeezing through the gaps or passing over hidden valleys, the air crossing mountain ranges has one further trick up its sleeve, a consequence of moisture being wrung out of rising air. Because the cooling rate of air from which water vapour is condensing is the SALR, moist air reaching the crest of a mountain range is relatively warm.

As it descends, it warms up, condensation ceases and the temperature rises at the DALR. The result is that the dry air descending on the leeward side can become remarkably warm (*see* Fig 4.8). Known as the föhn in the Alps and the chinook in the Rockies, this type of wind can have a disastrous impact on snow cover.

In the Alps the ideal conditions for the development of the föhn are when southerly winds bring warm, moist air from the Mediterranean. While this may produce heavy snow at the highest levels, on the northern flanks of the Alps it leads to a rapid thaw. The warm, dry air and fluctuating atmospheric pressure is enervating and widely attributed by the locals to all sorts of physical and mental disorders! The föhn is most likely to damage skiing conditions from the Bernese Oberland through southernmost Germany to the resorts at the northern edge of the Austrian Alps. By comparison, the impact on the French Alps is less marked, and for obvious reasons cooler air coming from the north does not have such an impact on the southern slopes of the Alps. This is also another reason why those resorts sheltered deep in the heart of the mountains – such as Val d'Isère, St Moritz and Obergurgl – fare much better than those on the edges.

The chinook in North America has the greatest impact on Alberta, where moist Pacific air crossing British Columbia can produce extraordinary changes in temperature on the eastern flanks of the Rockies. In part, this is because the warm air displaces frigid arctic air that often sits on the plains of Alberta and Saskatchewan. Stories of the temperature rising from $-20°C$ ($-4°F$) to $4°C$ ($39°F$) in less than five minutes are, however, part of the folklore of the region! Such extreme changes may only extend a relatively short distance beyond the mountains before the warm air glides up over the dense, cold,

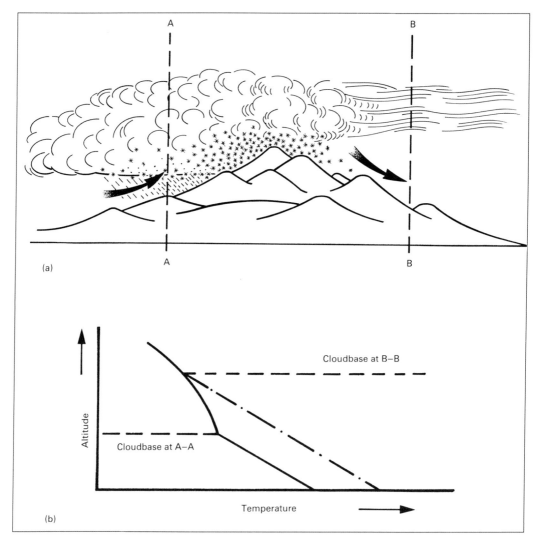

Fig 4.8 *How the föhn develops. Warm moist air that is forced to rise over a mountain range cools to form condensation (a). The consequent release of latent heat slows the rate of cooling with altitude (the continuous line in (b)), and when the now dry air descends on the leeward side of the range it warms more rapidly (the dash-dotted line in (b)).*

arctic air, but its impact on the snow cover in the resorts of Alberta is dramatic. Thick snow can melt away as if by magic in just a few hours at low levels.

5
Climatology

Moderation is a fatal thing.
Nothing succeeds like excess.
Oscar Wilde (1854–1900)

By now it should have become clear that two main principles affect mountain weather. First, mountains usually have more of almost everything – they are colder, wetter or snowier, and windier than the surrounding lowlands. The scale of these differences is easily overlooked, especially where mountains and major cities exist cheek by jowl – for example, it is easy to forget just how different the weather in Geneva or Salt Lake City is to that of the mountains a few hours' drive away. Second, mountains generate their own weather, so our experience of what happens in the lowlands may not be a reliable guide to experiences at higher levels. We therefore need some measure of what goes on in different mountain ranges in order to gain a reasonable guide as to what we are likely to experience from place to place.

A coherent picture of the conditions found in different regions must distinguish between weather and climate. Weather is what happens daily, while climate is the average of the weather over many years and climatology is the study of how and why the climate varies from place to place and season to season over longer timescales. By its very nature, climatology can only provide a general picture, for in practice the weather is hardly ever average but instead fluctuates about the norm. None the less, it is the norm which matters.

The first thing to do is to decide what features of the weather really matter in making your plans. It follows from the discussion in Chapters 2 and 3 that the combination of snowfall and temperature are most important for skiers, with sunshine also playing a major factor both in terms of enjoyment and quality of the snow. In practice, however, the amount of snowfall is notoriously difficult to measure accurately. Moreover, many of the figures published by resorts need to be treated with caution as information as to where and at what altitude they were recorded is often missing. There is also the implication that figures are sometimes designed to put the best gloss on a resort's conditions, an inevitable practice given the rivalry between resorts about claimed snowfall records. It is therefore far better to rely on meteorologically approved records produced by national weather services. Where the figures of these records differ appreciably from those produced by resorts, it is for you to choose on which you will place your trust.

Another reason for treating total snowfall figures with caution is that they are not particularly relevant if the snow is blown hither and thither or is subject to frequent freeze-thaw cycles. What really matters to skiers is the depth of the snowpack, and whenever possible snow-depth figures will be given.

However, unless good snow depths are accompanied by reasonable temperatures and adequate sunshine, few skiers will want to visit the resort. The statistics given in this book are therefore designed to consider the trade-off between the various meteorological elements and to see whether it is possible to achieve the ideal of an excess of both snow and sun. To do this, the emphasis will be on the needs of skiers as their interests are so sensitive to the weather. Climbers and walkers are less demanding, but the general statistics provide insights into what to expect throughout the winter.

Because many of the basic climatological statistics are much of a muchness, they are presented *en masse* in the Appendix. This avoids breaking up the text, and also makes it easier to compare different places. Instead, in this chapter a broad-brush approach is adopted to describe the winter weather in different mountain regions. Statistics for places named in the text which do not appear in the tables in this chapter can be found in the Appendix. Imperial units will appear alongside the metric values in the text for those of you who prefer them, but as these conversions would clutter things up too much in the tables and in the Appendix, here they contain only the metric values. The conversion factors for temperatures, altitudes, snowfall and snow depths are given in Table A.9.

THE ALPS

As noted in Chapter 1, the climatology statistics available for the Alps are more comprehensive than anywhere else, and enable us to draw up a more detailed range of conclusions about the region.

Temperature

For starters, the statistics confirm that it gets colder as you go higher. For the winter half of the year, the average temperature dips below 0°C (32°F) in late October at 2,000m (6,560ft) and stays well below freezing until early May. The −5°C (23°F) isotherm in January and February normally dips down to around 1,800m (5,900ft) in the French Alps and to around 1,500m (4,900ft) in Austria.

In terms of cold spells, the temperature at 2,500m (8,250ft) can be expected to fall to −20°C (−4°F) in January and February in most years, and on rare occasions to below −30°C (−22°F). At the highest levels, still lower figures can occur, but the data for Sonnblick at the eastern end of the Hohe Tauern range shows that it rarely ever falls below −30°C (−22°F) at around the 3,000m (10,000ft) level. Furthermore, even in May temperatures can fall well below −10°C (14°F) at night, so ski-tourers in late spring still need plenty of protective clothing. By comparison, daytime maxima are more difficult to interpret (*see* page 21), so for the moment, all that needs to be said is that for the winter half of the year (November to April) the shade temperature rarely rises above freezing at 2,500m (8,250ft).

Snowfall

Turning to snowfall figures (*see* Table 5.1), there are significant variations from place to place at resort level – say, 1,000–2,000m (3,300–6,600ft). At higher levels, the snowfall on average exceeds 1,000cm (400in), so the chances are that there will be reliable snow cover at these levels from December to May (*see* Table 5.2). Above about 3,000m (10,000ft), virtually all precipitation falls as snow (at Sonnblick in July and August, 65 per cent of the precipitation is snow), and the

Resort	Altitude (m)	A	S	O	N	D	J	F	M	A	M	J	J	Total (cm)
Engleberg	1,015	—	—	21	59	74	83	79	79	63	7	—	—	466
Leysin	1,330	—	1	28	63	90	89	86	90	58	8	—	—	513
Crans/Montana	1,505	—	1	18	62	112	109	101	75	39	6	1	—	524
Davos	1,580	1	8	38	72	95	93	85	82	61	23	5	1	562
Zermatt	1,630	—	1	7	41	80	40	48	44	30	10	4	—	303
Bever	1,700	—	4	19	52	50	58	49	46	30	11	1	—	319
Arosa	1,818	4	19	60	116	113	118	111	125	112	55	16	2	852
St Moritz	1,825	—	7	20	68	56	64	50	57	38	14	2	—	377
St Gotthard	2,095	4	21	56	189	144	129	150	117	140	68	15	6	1,037
Gütsch	2,287	12	37	94	186	192	173	200	217	228	114	40	7	1,500
Säntis	2,496	28	45	96	164	189	196	172	173	206	133	55	26	1,484
Weissfluhjoch	2,540	22	36	72	125	137	119	125	133	117	84	45	21	1,036

Swiss Snowfall Figures

Table 5.1

opportunities for summer skiing on the glaciers and ski-touring extend throughout most of the year.

Sunshine

A somewhat less expected result can be seen in the variations in sunshine throughout the year: while the lowlands are sunnier in summer, the uplands get more sun in the winter. This may seem odd when combined with the fact that the mountains also get more precipitation, and more precipitation usually means more cloud, but it will come as no surprise to anyone who has flown regularly into Geneva or Munich as the sunlit Alps can often be seen standing out clear above the murk which envelops the valleys. As a general figure, the upper levels of the Alps have bright sunshine for around 40 per cent of the daylight hours during winter and spring. This proportion does not vary appreciably from December to April, and the fact that the precipitation figures also remain steady shows there is no optimum time for reducing the chances of stormy weather or increasing the prospects of settled, sunny conditions.

Inversions

The reason for the surprisingly good sunshine figures is what is known as inversion. This phenomenon plays an important part in the meteorology of mountain regions and most frequently occurs in calm, anticyclonic conditions when radiation cooling at ground level and the drainage of cold air down into the valleys combine to reverse the normal vertical temperature profile (see Fig 5.1). The prevalence of these conditions in the vicinity of the Alps explains why the temperature lapse rate at lower levels in midwinter is rather less than the standard figures. It also explains why many skiers are so smug when, having spent a week in brilliant sunshine, they return to lower levels and discover that cloud or freezing fog has been the order of the day down in the valley.

The same phenomenon operates within the mountains. As a general rule, the tempera-

Snowdepths in the Alps during the Winter (cm)							
Resort	**Altitude**	**D**	**J**	**F**	**M**	**A**	**M**
AUSTRIA							
Kitzbühel	760	17	36	44	35	4	—
Waidring	770	30	51	66	52	12	—
Hochfilzen	960	40	73	93	68	20	—
Seefeld	1,190	28	51	64	51	15	—
St Anton	1,300	27	53	65	51	17	—
Galtür	1,590	36	62	84	71	34	5
Obergurgl	1,940	44	67	90	89	60	11
SWITZERLAND							
Engleberg	1,015	19	33	38	28	8	—
Leysin	1,330	23	38	52	42	19	1
Crans-Montana	1,505	34	58	86	69	33	1
Davos	1,580	40	63	80	80	45	5
Zermatt	1,630	37	57	65	58	20	1
Bever	1,700	39	64	80	70	34	2
Arosa	1,818	60	84	109	118	103	34
St Moritz	1,825	39	57	63	57	19	1
St Gotthard	2,095	132	181	209	226	230	166
Gütsch	2,287	128	173	233	280	319	260
Säntis	2,496	149	220	292	333	358	322
Weissfluhjoch	2,540	102	146	173	192	208	186
FRANCE							
Megève	1,113	28	47	61	30	8	—
Pralognan-la-Vanoise	1,420	52	79	100	93	61	10
St-Christophe-en-Osian	1,560	35	65	81	71	29	2
Mont Cenis	2,000	42	80	114	130	108	38
St Veran	2,040	33	60	74	64	24	2

Table 5.2

ture range from night to day in high mountain valleys is about twice the values recorded on the peaks. This is due to two principal effects. First, the peaks do not heat up as much as sheltered valleys during the day, even when all the area is cloaked in deep snow, and hence they remain at the temperature of the free atmosphere flowing through the mountains. Second, cooling air drains down the mountainside and collects in the valleys at night, especially in clear, calm, cold conditions.

Making Comparisons

Looking at the statistics in more detail reveals certain interesting features of the climatology of the Alps. The variations of temperature are relatively straightforward. The winter temperatures fall a bit as one goes eastwards and

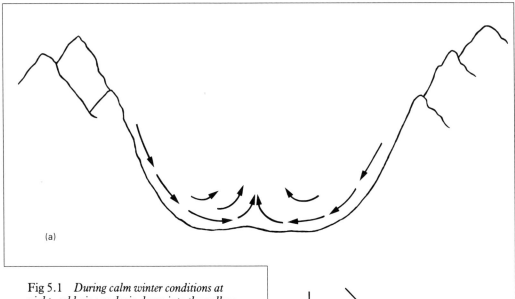

(a)

Fig 5.1   *During calm winter conditions at night, cold air can drain down into the valleys (a) and invert the normal temperature profile with altitude (b), so that the highest temperatures are found part of the way up the mountain.*

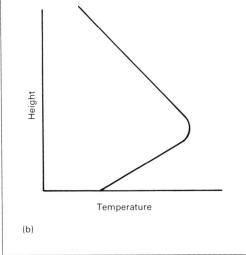

(b)

with it the snow-line descends to lower levels, so Austrian resorts at 800m (2,600ft) can offer skiing at a level which is not possible in the French Alps. The variations in the amount of snowfall and snow depths are much less easy to explain, and reflect the effects discussed in Chapter 4.

There is a range of more than a factor of two, at any given altitude, between the snowier and less well-endowed parts of the Alps. The best snow records are found in the French Alps from the Vanoise to the Mont Blanc massif, in central Switzerland from the St Gotthard Pass of the Glarner Alps through the Vorarlberg, and to the Kitzbüheler Alps in Austria. The regions of relatively low snowfall are found on the Italian side of the Maritime Alps and Parpaillon as far north as Bardonécchia, the Valais Alps around Zermatt, the Engadin around St Moritz, the Oetztal and the Dolomites. Other areas have intermediate snow records.

As Table 5.1 shows, this means that resorts such as Crans-Montana, Davos and Arosa get more snow than Zermatt or St Moritz. The figures for St Gotthard and Gütsch confirm what the *cognoscenti* have known for a long time, and that is that the snow record for

45

Andermatt has been almost unequalled among the traditional alpine resorts. The precipitation figures for Austria (*see* Appendix) confirm the dryness of the Oetztal (Vent), while the high values for Schmittehohe, above Zell am See, endorse the snowy reputation of the Hohe Tauern mountains. Similarly, the precipitation figures for French sites underpin the limited records for places such as Courcheval, La Plagne, and Val d'Isere/Tignes which suggest these resorts often have the heaviest and most reliable snowfall in the Alps.

Examination of the snow-depth figures (*see* Table 5.2) shows the same pattern, but some of the differences are less marked. So while Zermatt and St Moritz, on average, do not build up the same snowpack as Davos or Arosa, the differences are less noticeable than those for snowfall. This evening out of the figures may in part be explained by the sheltered position of the drier resorts (*see* page 36). The same applies to Obergurgl, whose snowfall record is on a par with Davos. For the rest, the snowpack figures at resort level show considerable uniformity, with Pralognan-la-Vanoise, St-Christophe-en-Osian (near les Deux Alpes), Crans-Montana, Galtür, St Anton, Seefeld and Waidring all being remarkably similar.

The other feature of the Austrian snow-depth figures is that they can be used to check the reputation of some famed 'snowcorners' (*Schneewinkel*). The figures show that Kitz-bühel does not look that special in this respect, and its seasonal snowfall of 284cm (113in) is typical for the north Tyrol at an altitude of around 750m (2,460ft). Better snowfall occurs around St Johann in Tirol, with both Waidring and Fieberbrunn having seasonal snowfall of about 450cm (180in). At Hochfilzen (just above Fieberbrunn) the annual figure is 634cm (250in), considerably more than falls at Obergurgl, nearly 1,000m (3,000ft) higher.

THE PYRENEES

The Pyrenees provide slightly different conditions from the Alps. Being a little further south and much closer to the Atlantic, they experience stormier and slightly warmer weather, so it is assumed that they have less reliable snow and a shorter skiing season. However, the mountains, stretching 450km (280 miles) from the Bay of Biscay to the Mediterranean and sporting more than eighty peaks over 3,000m (10,000ft), do offer plenty of exciting skiing.

It is not easy to sum up the climate of the Pyrenees in a few figures as the range marks a sharp transition in climate. Napoleon said that Africa starts at the Pyrenees, and climatically the mountains do represent a transition zone. This means that the variation in snowfall from the Atlantic to the Mediterranean ends of the mountains is substantial. Also, the variation between the French and Spanish sides is considerable, with the southern slopes being drier. The subject of amounts of snowfall in the Pyrenees is therefore a matter of fierce debate.

The winter temperatures for Bansol in Andorra at an altitude of 1,667m (5,477ft) are no lower than those of Lus-la-Croix-Haute in the French Alps between Grenoble and Gap at an altitude of only 1,037m (3,401ft). Similarly, the observatory at Pic du Midi at 2,883m (9,456ft) experiences temperatures that lie between the winter values for St Gotthard at 2,095m (6,872ft) and Säntis at 2,496m (8,187ft). So, you have to go some 500m (1,640ft) higher in the Pyrenees to get the same temperature.

The winter precipitation figures are on a par with the drier parts of the Alps at any given level. Qualitative evidence suggests that the snowfall on the northern slopes is more comparable with the wetter parts of the Alps. On the southern side, the precipitation is lower and more variable from year to year. The generally higher temperatures and the fact that much of the skiing is at a slightly lower altitude than many of the best-known resorts in the Alps means that it is not surprising that the snow records for the Pyrenees are less impressive. The seasons here are shorter and the risks of hitting a bad weather patch are higher than in the Alps.

THE SCOTTISH HIGHLANDS

The Scottish Highlands are given a separate billing for several reasons: first, they are an excellent example of the combination of the extremes of an oceanic climate with mountains; second, they have been the subject of more detailed meteorological studies than almost any other equivalent mountainous area; and finally, they are a mecca for a huge number of climbers, walkers and even some skiers from within the British Isles.

The fact that we have reliable climatological records for the highest altitudes in the Highlands (*see* Table A.2) is thanks to an intrepid band of Victorian scientists who maintained an observatory on the top of Ben Nevis (1,343m, or 4,403ft) between 1884 and 1903. The striking feature of the observations they made is that the winter temperatures are low – on a par with those at 1,800m (5,900ft) in the Alps. This is all the more remarkable because of the mildness found at low levels, and emphasizes the high lapse rate in such oceanic climates; the transition from mild lowlands to wintry Highlands is extremely rapid.

The precipitation levels in the Highlands are high, and concentrated in the winter half of the year. However, even in the depths of winter, some 20 per cent of the precipitation falls in the form of rain at the highest levels. The frequent freeze-thaw cycles produce the challenging snow and ice conditions that are so attractive to climbers, but which are a pain to many skiers and positively perilous to ill-equipped walkers. The average maximum snow depth observed at Ben Nevis was 221cm (87in) in mid-April, a figure that compares well with late-season figures at high levels in the Alps (*see* Table 5.2).

A more important feature of the Highlands is the windiness. In January 1983, the average wind-speed was 88km/h (55mph) on the 1,245m (4,084ft) peak of Cairngorm, this being equivalent to a continuous gale-force 9 wind throughout the whole month. The typical average January wind-speed for the summits of the Scottish Highlands is 32km/h (20mph).

This combination of heavy precipitation and high winds means that snow depths depend more on the combination of topography and wind direction than on the actual amount of snow that falls. Moreover, at lower levels in the Cairngorms, the temperature is barely cold enough to sustain reliable snow cover. The number of days with snow cover varies from just over fifty days at around 300m (1,000ft) to 220 days at around 1,200m (4,000ft). So, anyone wishing to ski above about 600m (2,000ft) needs to go where the snow has collected in appreciable drifts; this is best reflected in a combined measure of snow and wind, termed 'snowdrift'. The higher the combination of wind and snow, the greater the chance of appreciable and lasting accumulations forming on sheltered slopes where skiing facilities are usually sited. This observation also confirms the importance of that essential feature of Scottish skiing – snow fences which retain the snow in the vicinity of the runs.

The other major drawbacks to skiing in the Highlands are the high levels of cloudiness and the short days in midwinter. In December and January, the proportion of daylight hours that are sunny is a niggardly 15 per cent, the figure rising to around 25 per cent in March and April. When this is combined with the possibility of a mild start to the winter – as has so often been the case in recent years – reliable and more pleasant skiing may not occur until February or March. The fact that spring warms up very slowly, however, does mean that the best snow often occurs in April when the days are lengthening rapidly and the weather tends to be more settled than earlier in the year.

Other upland areas of the British Isles do not have sufficiently reliable snow cover to maintain viable skiing operations, but, as many hillwalkers know, there can often be exciting snow and ice conditions at higher levels. On average, British mountains have between twenty and thirty-five days of snow cover at around 300m (1,000ft). This figure rises to between 75 and 120 days at 1,000m (3,000ft), with the lower figures representing conditions on the more westerly peaks.

THE REST OF EUROPE

Covering the rest of Europe in one go is no easy matter as significant mountain chains lie scattered from northern Norway to the Peloponnese, from the Sierra Nevada to the Caucasus, and, if we stretch a point, to eastern Turkey. Here we will concentrate on two aspects: first, the scope of Scandinavia and, in particular, Norway; secondly, the opportunities for winter sports that are developing in Central Europe, down into Romania, Bulgaria and on into Turkey.

Norway

The Lillehammer Winter Olympics held in February 1994 provided a timely reminder of the attractions of Norwegian skiing. Thanks to the combined effects of recent ice ages, Norway, like Scotland, is not blessed with high alpine peaks, but with more modest, eroded mountains. Also like Scotland, it experiences an oceanic climate with prevailing westerly winds, which, when combined with its high latitude (60°N to 63°N), undermines the charms of its skiing. However, the contrast from the west coast to the inland areas is striking as the weather becomes markedly colder and drier, with the interior having conditions that are more continental than those in Scotland. For example, Geilo and Lillehammer are much colder and drier than, say, Bergen. This means that Norwegian resorts can exploit the height range of the mountains to the full, and also get more sunshine and less wind. The conditions are therefore more nearly on a par with New England (see page 53) than Scotland, but with far fewer daylight hours and less sunshine in midwinter. As is the case with New England, inland Norway can also experience bitterly cold conditions. Even during February 1994, the month of the Winter Olympics, which was not considered exceptionally cold, the lowest temperature in Oslo, let alone out on the mountains, was −27.5°C (−17.5°F).

All of this tends to confirm the general view that Norway is much better for cross-country than downhill skiing. However, if the Alps are having a bad year the chances are that the lower temperatures and wetter climate in Norway will produce good snow conditions, in some resorts.

Central and Eastern Europe

During the worst drought years in the Alps, it was claimed that the future lay further east. By the time you reach Poprad in Slovakia – the base camp for skiing the High Tatras – the temperatures have fallen significantly. With skiing to about 2,600m (8,500ft), there is considerable potential here, but this has yet to be developed significantly. The same probably does not apply to the mountains on the Czech–Polish border, even though, as the figures for Sniezka show, the conditions are right for reliable snow.

Heading south and east does not produce much advantage. In Romania, there is skiing up to about 2,400m (7,900ft) in the Carpathians. The winter climate for Brasov is similar to that around Innsbruck, so the snow conditions will be comparable to those in many of the Austrian resorts. Similarly, in Bulgaria the figures for Sofia are in the same ballpark, so in the Rila Alps, just to the south of the capital city, skiing is at 1,320–2,540m (4,330–8,830ft) and the snow conditions are, if anything, more reliable. To conclude, there are few climatological reasons for choosing these central and East European resorts in preference to the Alps. So, given that many of these more eastern areas have yet to be developed to any degree, they only represent better skiing prospects when the weather patterns bring a drought to the western end of the Alps, with low-pressure systems either moving up into the Balkans from the Mediterranean or down from Scandinavia.

While the occurrence of this type of pattern brings somewhat better conditions to eastern Europe, it results in much heavier snow in Turkey. Given the extent of the mountains in this country, there is considerable potential for skiing. At present, most of the limited skiing can be found south of Istanbul or on the very snowy mountains behind Antalya, where in spring you can take your pick between the beach or skiing, the two activities being available within a few hours' drive of one another. However, to get the full benefit of the heavy falls further east during the years when Europe is covered by an anticyclone across from the Azores, head for the mountains around Erzurum. Not only does

eastern Turkey have a climate similar to that of the southern Rockies (compare the figures for Erzurum with those for Aspen), but when this pattern prevails, Turkey gets higher than average snowfall. So, if the concerns about global warming (see page 65) are justified, then this may be an area with a future.

THE ROCKIES

Here the Rockies will be defined as covering the mountains that lie between New Mexico and Alberta, including those of Utah, Idaho and eastern British Columbia. This is a huge region including mountain ranges that cover an area some four times that of the Alps, and extending from 36°N to around 54°N. This means that the mountains experience a wide range of climatic conditions, but even so they can be treated in a reasonably consistent manner. Broadly speaking, in midwinter they are colder, drier and sunnier than the Alps, and because of this the ski areas that pepper these mountains are set at altitudes that provide the right combination of reliable snow and acceptable temperatures. So, with the tree-line descending from 3,200m (10,500ft) in New Mexico to about 2,100m (6,900ft) around Jasper, the altitude of ski resorts tends to drop as you travel northwards.

Temperature

The average temperatures in January and February throughout the Rockies are, in general, lower than those of the Alps – at resort level they range from −10°C (14°F) to −7°C (19°F), dropping even further in Canada. Comparable values in the Alps are found at the 2,000–3,000m (6,600–10,000ft) level, this covering the middle or upper slopes of many resorts. Furthermore, the temperatures can plunge far lower than in the

Alps: figures for Jackson, Wyoming, show that the lowest temperature recorded during the period from 1951 to 1980 was a numbing −46°C (−50°F). However, as the season advances the Rockies warm up more rapidly, and in the summer temperatures are considerably higher than those in the Alps. So, in March and April the daytime conditions are pleasantly warm and the sunshine figure is around 50 per cent of daylight hours.

These low temperatures mean that much of the skiing in the Rockies is down among the trees. This has two important benefits: first, the trees provide valuable shade in spring for more southerly resorts; second, they offer shelter from the cold during colder weather. The normal daytime highs in many places are reasonable, but the daily range is large, and when arctic air engulfs the mountains then it is time not only to don face masks and long johns but also to exploit any shelter there is to be had.

Precipitation

The precipitation figures of the Rockies are less easily summarized; the region covers such a wide area that there are bound to be significant differences. It is, however, possible to extract a considerable amount of information from the data given in the Appendix.

The amount of precipitation in the winter half of the year in the Colorado and Wyoming resorts is comparable to that of the drier parts of the Alps, such as the Engadin and the Oetztal (compare Bever and Vent in Table A.1 with Aspen, Crested Butte, Jackson and Steamboat Springs in Table A.5). The same applies to resorts in Alberta, such as Jasper and Lake Louise. In snowier areas, such as Silver Lake Brighton in Utah, Summit in Montana and Glacier National Park in British Columbia, precipitation figures are of the same order as those for Andermatt and major

French resorts above about 1,500m (4,900ft), but not as substantial as the figures for the snowiest high-altitude sites such as St Gotthard and Santis.

Making comparisons of snowfall is less easy. The fact that quantities increase rapidly with altitude, especially in Colorado (*see* page 16), means that the figures recorded in the resorts may understate the conditions on the slopes more than is the case for comparable sites in the Alps. As a general rule, the resorts claim 600–1,000cm (240–400in) of snowfall at skiing levels, with the best – such as Alta, Utah – reaching levels as high as 1,400cm (550in). The values quoted in Table 5.3 confirm these claims, at the same time showing that snowfalls at resort level can be much less – for example, in the case of Jackson. The figures for Silver Lake Brighton, Utah, confirm the fact that Cottonwood canyons have an extraordinary capacity to generate extra snowfall, while the high values for Wolf Creek Pass, Colorado, even allowing for its altitude, show that the San Juan Mountains get more than their fair share of snow.

Further north, the impact of the major depression track running along the United States–Canadian border (*see* page 27) is apparent in the high snowfall figures for Glacier National Park in the Selkirk Range. Over all, the amounts are, however, lower than the values of the coastal ranges of western North America, while their water equivalent (which defines depth of snowpack) is markedly lower.

Making Comparisons

When it comes to making comparisons between the Rockies and the Alps, it is important to consider both snowfall and water equivalent. There is also little point in comparing figures for the Rockies with those of the lower alpine resorts as there is no contest. What we are concerned about here is whether Alta, Aspen, Breckenridge, Jackson and Lake Louise offer better overall conditions than Val d'Isère, Verbier or Zermatt. The closest analogue in terms of temperature and snowfall at resort level in Colorado or Wyoming is Vent in the Oetztal, so anyone who has skied at Obergurgl will have a pretty good idea of what to expect in the southern Rockies. The same is also true of Zermatt.

When it comes to the snowier high French and Swiss resorts, the snowfall figures are on a par with Utah, Montana and the Canadian Rockies, and tend to have a higher water equivalent and hence a deeper base. However, this means on average that they get wetter snow. In summary, there is not much to choose between the two regions in terms of quantity. However, if you are after champagne powder there is a much higher chance of getting it in the Rockies; the price you pay is that it can sometimes be extremely cold, especially from Wyoming northwards.

It follows from this that deciding when the Rockies are a better bet than the Alps will depend more on which area is likely to have the best season. Unfortunately, the weather patterns of the Rockies are particularly difficult to classify because the mountains often act as the fulcrum for shifts in global circulation (see page 35), and hence the fluctuations in their weather do not follow any well-established rules. Indeed, attempts to produce winter forecasts, which have had some success in parts of the eastern United States, have proved to be completely worthless over the Rockies. It is better to rely instead on climatology. The safest course is to go to the snowier resorts in March when the risk of intensely cold weather is declining. But, as in the Alps, there is no pronounced pattern of either increased storminess or more settled weather in any particular month between December and April.

WESTERN NORTH AMERICA – MAMMOTH TO ALASKA

This region covers another huge stretch of mountains. For downhill skiers the important part is from Mammoth in the southern Sierra Nevada to Whistler and Blackcomb just north of Vancouver. Although there is a significant ski resort at Aleyeska, 65km (40 miles) south-east of Anchorage, for the most part the mountains of northern British Columbia, Alaska and the Yukon are the province of ski-tourers and mountaineers. Moreover, in places the mountains are home to both glaciers that reach down to the sea and permanent icefields at altitudes over 5,000m (16,400ft), all in the space of a few tens of kilometres. Such a wide range of conditions over so short a distance cannot easily be encapsulated in simple statistics.

Whatever the reasons for visiting these mountains, the most important factor in the winter half of the year is the vast amounts of snow that fall here. The depressions sweeping in from the North Pacific (see page 35) cause the weather to be predominantly stormy. This ensures that average snowfall figures around the tree-line are in the range of 1,000 –1,500cm (400–600in) over the complete extent of the coastal ranges (see Table 5.3). Much of this snow is heavy and wet, especially at lower levels. So, while resorts build up prodigious bases during the season, there is often no appreciable let-up in the weather to allow skiers to enjoy the conditions. As anyone who has skied when heavy snow is falling in the Cascades will know, not only is the visibility nil in such conditions, but the one manoeuvre you never try in knee-deep, new, sticky snow is the snowplough. Just how heavy this snow can be is shown in Table 5.3. The total accumulation of 28.5m (93ft) for the Paradise Ranger Station on Mount Rainier in 1971/2 is a world record for any

Resort	Altitude (m)	S	O	N	D	J	F	M	A	M	J	Total (cm)
Lake Placid, NY	366	—	3	43	58	62	64	62	26	4	—	320
Mt Washington, NH	1,909	—	10	45	74	102	100	108	52	9	—	499
Ste-Agathe-des-Monts, QUE	399	—	8	41	92	82	85	66	20	4	—	396
Silver Lake Brighton, UT	2,652	7	46	111	147	151	152	159	102	31	10	916
Wolf Creek Pass, CO	3,244	5	45	101	146	203	178	203	145	14	1	1,036
Jackson, WY	1,904	—	3	24	55	59	35	30	15	3	1	224
Glacier (Rogers Pass), BC	1,323	1	53	165	222	226	165	106	50	8	—	996
Glacier (Mt Fidelity), BC	1,969	19	124	255	286	259	215	181	117	46	15	1,518
Soda Springs, CA	2,100	5	36	93	170	232	188	166	68	39	9	1,012
Crater Lake, OR	1,974	8	51	139	248	268	234	194	106	51	6	1,305
Paradise, Mt Rainier, WA	1,655	8	52	164	252	306	227	251	124	50	10	1,444
Paradise, Mt Rainier, WA (1971/2)	1,655	23	149	311	577	704	404	278	364	20	13	2,850
Garibaldi, BC	381	—	7	46	120	151	81	61	12	—	—	478
Yakutat, AK	9	—	13	44	120	92	107	108	41	1	—	526

North American Snowfall Figures

Table 5.3

meteorological site, and by March 1972 the snowpack was recorded as being 9.32m deep (30ft). The precipitation and snowfall figures for Garibaldi in British Columbia, just below Blackcomb and Whistler, confirm that these resorts have similar heavy snowfalls. But at this level (381m, or 1,250ft) half the precipitation falls as rain even in December and January. So, especially in February and March, rain can often spoil the skiing below about 1,000m (3,300ft).

At the southern end of the Sierra Nevada and on the leeward side around Lake Tahoe, there are sufficient settled periods to ensure that full advantage can be made of the plentiful snow. The average sunshine figures in January and February are around 35 per cent, and the daytime temperatures are pleasantly high. Despite the southerly latitude, however, the regions can still experience very cold conditions. In Oregon, the best-known resort is Mount Bachelor, offering the compromise of high snowfall and moderate sun-

shine figures. In March, as the storm tracks move northwards, the conditions improve and so this is the best time for a visit. This combination means that the Californian resorts are then difficult to beat in providing the right mix of sun and snow.

Up around Seattle and Vancouver, settled weather is less frequent and so choosing the right week for a holiday can be more of a gamble. Sunshine figures are only about 20 per cent of daylight hours in January and February. Statistics for Vancouver show that roughly one winter in six has no settled cold spells lasting forty-eight hours or more, but in extreme years settled weather can hold sway for three weeks or more. These cold, clear bouts of weather are most likely to occur in January; they are uncommon in early December and late February, but pick up a bit in March. While these periods do not produce exceptionally cold weather near the coast (the temperature in Vancouver hardly ever falls as low as −15°C, or 5°F), further inland, behind the protecting coastal ranges, temperatures can plummet below −30°C (−22°F). So, while the best time for settled conditions is January, the choice is between milder but snowy and windy weather or bitter chill with brilliant sunshine – a happy medium is harder to find.

Fluctuations in snowfall are linked to wider patterns. When a blocking anticyclone forms off the coast of Oregon, the depressions sweep up towards Alaska. California will be hardest hit at such times, with snowfall in the mountains way below normal – as in the drought years of 1976/7 and 1980/1. In other years the pattern drives depressions further south, when many more storms hit California and good snow years ensue. It therefore pays to know what type of year it is going to be in the Sierra Nevada (see page 67). The consequences for the Coast Ranges of Washington State and British Columbia when a block forms are less profound, because there is almost always sufficient snow in all but the driest years – the problem here is more likely to be too much snow!

NEW ENGLAND AND EASTERN CANADA

The keyword for winter weather on the east coast of North America is variability. It is, however, a different kind of variability to that experienced in the gales and storms of the Scottish Highlands, taking instead the form of extraordinary fluctuations in temperature. The reason is that the entire region is a meteorological battleground. Invasions of intensely cold air sweep down suddenly from the Arctic, sometimes reaching as far south as Florida; equally rapidly, warm, humid air can flood north from the Gulf of Mexico, on occasions reaching as far north as Quebec. For the ski resorts of the region, stretching

from North Carolina to Quebec, this switchback weather poses peculiar challenges, with plentiful snow experiencing sudden and dramatic thaws followed by deep freezes. Before the days of artificial snow, east coast resorts were notorious for their rock-hard clear-blue ice, which could turn modest blue runs into terrifying ordeals.

It is best to concentrate on the region of New England across to Lake Placid in New York and up to Mont Tremblant in Quebec. This encompasses most of the serious skiing on the east coast and represents a manageable range of weather.

Figures for Mount Washington show a number of striking features of this climate. First, in spite of its lower altitude and latitude, the region is markedly colder in winter than much higher sites in the Alps, such as Sonnblick. When these figures are combined with the observations on temperature fluctuations, it can be seen that there are bouts of numbingly cold weather – having skied in Vermont in strong winds and a temperature of −30°C (−22°F), I can vouch for how painful such conditions can be. Further north, at Mont Tremblant, the temperatures can drop below −40°C (−40°F), and that is too cold. A friend who skied there in the late 1960s when the temperatures were this low explained that the only way to ensure your car started in the morning was to leave it idling all night; it used up two-thirds of a tank of gasoline, but it worked!

The next point to note is that there is plentiful precipitation and hence adequate snowfall at higher levels. At the base-level of many resorts – 300–500m (1,000–1,640ft) – the average snowfall is in the range of 250–400cm (100–160in) per year (see Table 5.3). However, the frequent thaws and occasional rains make artificial-snow production essential for reliable and acceptable skiing. The overall low temperatures mean, however, that snow-making facilities are widespread. Conversely, the high summer temperatures mean that virtually all the mountains lie below the tree-line; only Sugarloaf in Maine offers a skiable snowfield above the trees. These are therefore skiers' mountains, with shelter in cold weather and masses of high-quality cross-country trials. For the most part the mountains do not offer demanding climbing, and neither do they offer panoramic vistas as the only hillwalking is among the trees.

THE REST OF THE WORLD

To attempt to cover the climatology of mountains throughout the rest of the world is a tall order. The scope is immense, covering all of Asia, South America and Australasia, not to mention the permanent ice-caps of Antarctica and Greenland. Instead, we will concentrate on the most important skiing areas, giving only limited coverage to those areas that have yet to be developed or that remain the almost exclusive province of climbers. This means that we will look at the climates of southern South America, New Zealand and Japan, but will pass over the Himalayas and all other areas that have yet to be developed, as well as places such as Australia that have many dedicated local skiers, but whose conditions do not warrant travelling far to enjoy (*see* Thredbo, Table A.8).

South America

The potential of Chile and Argentina has been recognized for a number of years. In many respects, the conditions here are virtually a mirror-image of those described for western North America. Working on the basis of a simple rule of thumb that the stronger circulation in the southern hemisphere shifts the climatic zones some five degrees of latitude towards the Equator, it can be assumed that the Andes behind Santiago (33°S) have a climate similar to that of the southern Sierra Nevada around Mammoth (*see* Christo Redentor, Table A.8). Furthermore, although the variations in global circulation patterns are less pronounced than in the northern hemisphere, the fluctuations in snowfall from year to year are dramatic at these low latitudes (*see* page 67).

Further south, Chilean resorts such as Villarrica have conditions which are more akin to the Cascades, while further south again, the snowfall is substantial and the mountains are dominated by major icefields which stretch from 46°S to 51°S. At these latitudes the strong westerly patterns in winter mean that the weather is almost unremittingly stormy. This is a desolate, windswept region where the average summer temperatures at an altitude of 2,000m (6,600ft) are −2 to −5°C (28–23°F) and in winter −7 to −10°C (19–14°F). Only the most intrepid, who wish to tackle such ultimate mountaineering challenges as the Towers of Paine, venture into this icy wilderness.

There is one other interesting feature of how the Andes interact with strong zonal circulation in the southern hemisphere. Because the mountain range is both high and narrow, it has a less diverting effect than the more extensive mountains in North America and, as a result, casts a more dramatic rain shadow. Precipitation figures along the ridge-line of the Andes around 40°S are over 3,000mm (120in), but fall to a tenth of this figure at an altitude of 1,000m (3,300ft) on the leeward side. This means that the snow-fall on the Argentinian side is much less than in Chile, and that resorts such as Las Lenas (about 200km, or 125 miles, south-south-east of Santiago) and Bariloche (further south still) sit above a virtual desert landscape.

New Zealand

The Southern Alps, in the South Island of New Zealand, stretch from 41°S to 47°S, their seasonal snow cover extending to 50,000 sq km (20,000 sq miles). On the western flanks of these mountains, which in general rise to 2,000m (6,600ft) and in the central part exceed 3,000m (10,000ft) (Mount Cook is 3,763m, or 12,343ft, high) there are copious quantities of rainfall and snowfall (rainfall equivalents exceed 10,000mm, or 394in in places) and substantial glaciers. On the eastern side of the mountains the precipitation is much lower. The average winter snow-line runs from around 1,000m (3,000ft) in the south, to about 1,300m (4,300ft) in the north. As elsewhere in the southern hemisphere, winds are a major feature of the weather at these latitudes.

The lack of early economic activity in the mountains means that there are few meteorological records (apart from those for Ski Basin) to provide insights into conditions in the mountains. However, the figures for Lake Tekapo, gateway to the Godley Glacier, are a guide to the conditions of both this area and of the nearby resort of Mount Hutt, whose windiness is encapsulated in the soubriquet, 'Mount Shutt'. Similarly, Manorburn Dam figures give a measure of the climate in the Wanaka/Queenstown area below the Mount Aspiring National Park, home to the Tyndall Glacier and the Harris Mountains, with their magnificent heliskiing. As elsewhere, the fluctuations from year to year are considerable in spite of high snowfall figures. None the less, the South Island of New Zealand, together with Chile, offers the most exciting, extensive and reliable skiing in the southern hemisphere.

Japan

The inclusion of Japan in this section is justified on two grounds: first, the country's resorts attract a huge number of skiers (over 12 million at the last count); second, the mountains have an interesting climatology. The latter produces some particularly interesting skiing conditions, while the former results in massive queues.

Although sometimes defined as an oceanic climate, Japan's winter weather bears more resemblance to the east coast of North America, with one important difference. The Sea of Japan both ameliorates the temperature of the icy winds that frequently stream out of Siberia, and at the same time picks up huge amounts of moisture. The effect of this is that even places at sea-level in Hokkaido, such as Sapporo, which hosted the Winter Olympics in 1972, can be bitterly cold, as the figures for Rusutsu indicate. The temperatures are more moderate in the mountains of Honshu (see Tajima in Table A.7), where the 1998 Winter Olympics will be held, but the winter precipitation figures are higher than for the east coast of the United States. When this is combined with the fact that the mountains in central Honshu rise to over 3,000m (10,000ft), the result is prodigious snow depths. Moreover, the exceedingly cold Siberian air means that much of this snow falls as high-quality light, dry powder.

6
Weather Forecasting

Mais où sont les neiges d'antan?
(*Where are the snows of yesteryear?*)
François Villon (b 1431)

The essence of forecasting is that analysis of past changes and current conditions can provide guidance of what is to come. This is particularly true of mountain meteorology. On every timescale, from the imperceptibly slow but massive changes over the centuries associated with the advance and retreat of glaciers, to the sudden shifts that can envelope a sun-drenched mountain in freezing cloud, driving snow and squally winds in a matter of minutes, variations in the weather dominate our enjoyment of the mountains. The more we can anticipate how the weather will change, the greater will be our chances of getting the best out of our time in the mountains. However, this requires us to know something not only of the long-term changes and what weather forecasts are capable of doing, but also how to read the signs of changing conditions on the spot. To do this we need first to go back into the past.

GLACIERS COME AND GLACIERS GO

The movement of glaciers has exercised a peculiar fascination over scientists and historians seeking to understand the nature of climatic change, at the same time having a much greater impact on those who have lived in their shadow. Records have therefore been kept of times when glaciers surged down into the valleys where people lived. In addition, scientists have measured the age of debris left in the terminal moraines which mark the furthest extent of glaciers down mountains. This combination of historical records and scientific studies produces a consistent picture: between the mid-16th and mid-19th centuries, the world's glaciers were more extensive than they have been in the current century. Even more striking is the scale of retreat that took place world-wide during the first half of the 20th century.

Anyone who has skied the Vallée Blanche above Chamonix may be surprised to learn that in the 1640s and again in the 1820s the Mer de Glace extended down to the floor of the Arve valley. Considering the glacier now ends more than a kilometre back up its valley, this provides a good measure of how much more extensive it was in the past. Most skiers today content themselves with taking the train down from Montenvers rather than choosing to walk back to Chamonix with their skis as there is often no snow cover below the snout of the glacier. In recent decades the movement of glaciers in many parts of the world has been complicated with successive retreats and advances, but in no case have the advances come anywhere near to recouping the losses that took place earlier this century.

The importance of these observations for mountain meteorology is that the changes have been linked to general global warming since the mid-19th century (*see* Fig 6.1). Since the standard forecast of the impact of man-made pollution on the greenhouse effect predicts a further appreciable warming in the coming decades, the impact on the world's glaciers and, by implication, their associated snow and icefields is substantial. It is therefore interesting to explore the link between the behaviour of glaciers and general climate in a bit more detail as it is of direct relevance to understanding possible future changes in the mountains.

Glacial Statistics

The most comprehensive studies of both the fluctuations in glacial extent and associated changes in the climate have been conducted in Switzerland. The period of advancing glaciers from around AD1550 to 1850 – generally known as the Little Ice Age – was marked by significant movements of the glaciers. Detailed analyses of the weather prepared by Christian Pfister at the University of Berne, who has collected a huge range of climatic data based on observations of such events as the annual flowering and fruiting dates of many plants and trees, wine harvest dates and the incidence of frost, snow and ice, indicate that during this period winters were on average around 0.6°C (1.1°F) cooler, springs and autumns were about 0.3°C (0.5°F) cooler, while summer temperatures were virtually the same as they are now. However, when the shorter term fluctuations are examined, the most marked glacial advances – such as those in the 1590s, 1690s and 1810s – are seen to coincide with periods of cool, wet summers. By comparison, variations in winter have had less impact and, indeed, milder but wetter

winters also replenished the glaciers. In spring and autumn the conclusions are the same. Late-spring and early autumn snows had a positive effect, while dry, warm weather led to rapid retreat.

The same story emerges in the 20th century (*see* Fig 6.2), with the prolonged period of retreat being interrupted by the cool, wet summers of the 1910s and 1920s, and those of the 1970s and early 1980s. These historical results are broadly consistent with the wider picture that has been built up around the world during the 20th century. It is the periods with below-average precipitation and above-average temperatures during the summer half of the year that lead to the most rapid retreat of glaciers. In places where warmer winters lead to a significant shift in the balance of precipitation falling as rain rather than snow, the retreat can be attributed to more general warming. In general, however, the changes in temperature during the winter half of the year in mid- and high latitudes have played a less important part in the movement of glaciers. This is an interesting conclusion as the prospect of global warming has been seen by many skiers as the 'spectre at the feast' in recent years. Therefore, evidence of how the amount of snow and the duration of snow cover is linked to global warming is of central interest to skiers.

SNOW COVER AND DEPTH RECORDS

Switzerland

Starting with Switzerland, winter snow cover has been recorded at Bever (altitude 1,710m, or 5,600ft) near St Moritz since 1880. Observations provide a measure of the length of the skiing season, since the number of days when snow lies at this level provides a reasonable

IPCC combined land and sea surface temperature anomaly 1860–July 1994 (with respect to 1951–80).

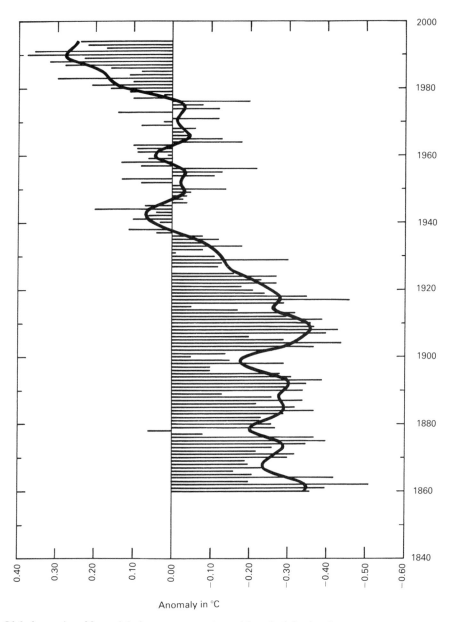

Anomaly in °C

Fig 6.1 *Global warming. Mean global temperature estimated from both land and sea observations shows a rise of about 0.5°C (0.9°F) over the last century. (Reproduced with permission of the Hadley Centre for Climate Prediction and Research, Bracknell.)*

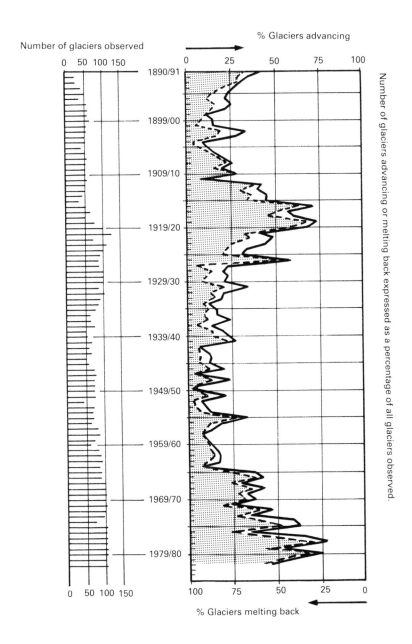

Fig 6.2   *Fluctuations of glacier snouts in the Swiss Alps between 1891 and 1982.*
(Reproduced with permission of Dr C Pfister.)

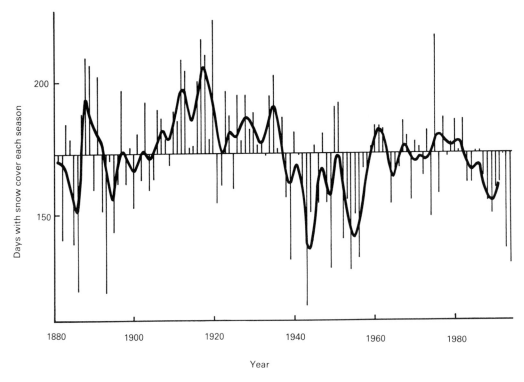

Fig 6.3   *The length of the season in the Engadin – the number of days with snow cover from August to July (the year is defined as that in which January fell) at Bever, near St Moritz, from 1880 to 1980, and then at nearby Samedan since 1980 (the smooth line shows longer term variations).*

insight to conditions at higher levels. The Bever record (*see* Fig 6.3) shows that since 1880 there has been no single appreciable trend, but instead there have been substantial changes from year to year and from decade to decade. For example, the number of days of snow cover were high in the 1910s, while the 1940s and 1950s featured short seasons by comparison.

These variations mirror in part the advances and retreats of Swiss glaciers (*see* Fig 6.2), the periods of glacial advance coinciding with the longest snow seasons. These snowy years were also marked by either cool, snowy autumns and/or springs. Whatever the winter

weather, there was snow cover at Bever virtually every year from mid-December to the end of March, with the deepest snow occurring around the end of February (*see* Table 5.2).

The variations in snow cover from year to year are striking, with the number of days ranging from less than four months (115 days in 1942/3) to well over seven months (223 days in 1919/20) when cover was continuous from the beginning of October to well into May. While there are runs of snowy or less snowy years, there is no clear pattern, and adjacent years can switch from dearth to abundance with the length of the season

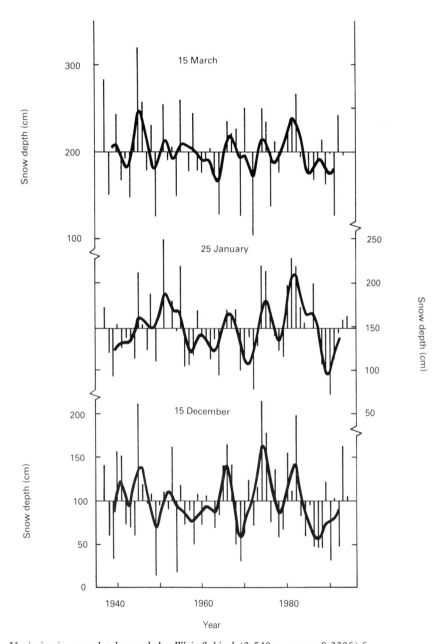

Fig 6.4 *Variation in snow depth recorded at Weissfluhjoch (2,540 metres, or 8,330ft) for each winter since 1936/7 for three dates (15 December observations are shown as the same year as the subsequent January and March figures for each season). The figures show how the amount of snow fluctuated from year to year and within each season (the smooth lines show the longer term fluctuations).*

varying by up to two months. The absence of cycles, in spite of what look tantalizingly like periodicities in the smoothed record, must be underlined. This is a well-known feature of all meteorological records: whenever a reliable cycle seems to appear and is used to forecast future fluctuations, it promptly disappears! So, rummaging around in the snow statistics to look for patterns that may be used to draw conclusions about future seasons is a waste of time.

The same story emerges from measurements of snow depth. The record kept by the Swiss Institute for Snow and Avalanche Research at Weissfluhjoch above Davos since 1936 is illuminating (*see* Fig 6.4). The figures at an altitude of 2,540m (8,330ft) are representative of the upper slopes of skiing resorts in the Alps. On average, these figures show that there is over 1m (39in) of snowpack

from mid-December until well beyond the end of April, with the deepest snow (210cm, or 83in) occurring, on average, in mid-April (*see* Fig 6.5). This means that while the snow depth builds up through the season, the variation from year to year remains roughly constant. If you are looking for reliable snow it is therefore better to go later in the season – providing you enjoy spring snow conditions (*see* page 22). Indeed, the deepest snow accumulates even later at the highest levels – at the Sonnblick Observatory in Austria, at an altitude of 3,080m (10,102ft), the mean date of maximum snow cover is 29 April. This explains why the *aficionados* of spring skiing and high-level touring claim that the best conditions are found in May, when the crowds have disappeared and new falls of snow on a deep base can provide a magical, if short-lived skiing experience (*see* Fig 6.6).

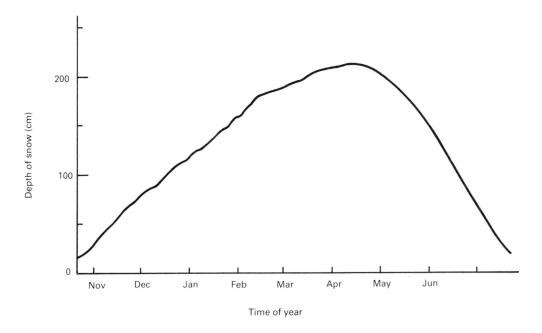

Fig 6.5 *The average snow depth recorded at Weissfluhjoch (2,540 metres, or 8,330ft) during the season, showing that maximum depth is recorded in mid-April.*

Fig 6.6 *Snow in May. The Solaise 'bumps' at Val d'Isère sporting a fine new coat of snow on 3 May 1993. (Photograph by John Yates-Smith, reproduced with permission of YSE Limited.)*

As for trends throughout the season, there has been no significant change in snow depths over the last six decades; instead, the same fluctuations on every timescale emerge. Not only are there runs of good and bad years and sudden switches from year to year, but there can also be marked changes in fortune within seasons. Some years get off to a bad start, only to pick up well (for example, 1991/2), while others can make a reasonable start, only to tail off badly (for example, 1990/1). In general, however, those that get off to a really good start (for example, 1973/4, 1974/5 and 1981/2) maintain good snow throughout the season, even though the core of the winter may be very mild, as was the case in both 1973/4 and 1974/5. Furthermore, there are surprisingly few instances of consistently thin snow throughout the whole season – the only three years with snow depths well below average from mid-December to mid-March during the last fifty-eight years were 1948/9, 1968/9 and 1971/2. Even the fabled dry year of 1963/4 got off to a moderate start at Weissfluhjoch, although available records do support the popular view that over all it was indeed the worst 'in living memory'. The consistent feature of these poor winters was not that they were particularly mild, but that they were very dry.

Austria

Records for Austria, some of which go back to 1895, convey the same message as the Swiss statistics. They confirm that the greatest fluctuations in duration of snow cover and depth are at altitudes below about 1,250m (4,100ft). In addition, they show that the variations from place to place in any one season can be striking. The figures for the combination of length of season and average snow depth for Jochberg, just above Kitzbühel, show a range of more than a factor of ten between the best and worst years (1943/4 and 1989/90 respectively), but no trend (*see* Fig 6.7). Moreover, there is a peak in the 1940s that is in marked contrast to snow cover figures for Bever in the same year. This means that the north-eastern corner of the Alps got much better snow in these years than

the more sheltered Engadin. So, for late bookers it pays to check the snow reports before choosing where to go as it can make all the difference, especially in the years with poor snow. Broadly speaking, either the east or west end of the Alps will get better conditions, or, less frequently, the southern flanks will do better than the northern slopes.

Although such lengthy statistical records are not available for other mountain regions, the same general principles apply. As a result, a number of useful guide-lines can be drawn up from these observations to help in planning a holiday.

1. There has been no significant trend in either the duration of snow cover or snow depth in the Alps for at least the last fifty years.
2. The most reliable snow cover at high

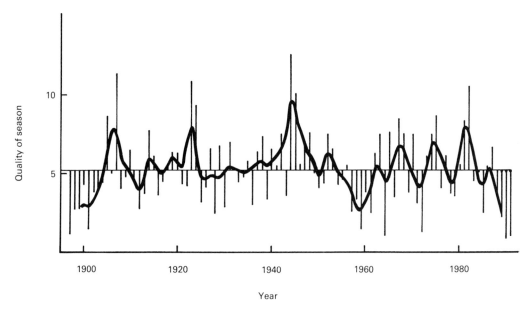

Fig 6.7 *The snow records for Jochberg, near Kitzbühel (1,000m, or 3,280ft), showing the good and bad years since 1896. The quality of each season is measured by the product of the length of the season in terms of days of snow cover and average snow depth over the season (the smooth line shows longer term variations).*

levels (around 2,500m, or 8,250ft, in the Alps) is found from mid-March to late April, while at resort level (around 1,500m, or 4,900ft, in the Alps) the deepest snow occurs in February.

3. There have been runs of good and bad years, but there have been no sustained patterns which could be used with any confidence to predict future seasons.

4. In spite of the longer term fluctuations, good and bad years can sometimes run back to back, so having an exceptional season is neither a guarantee that the next one will be in the same mould, nor that it will redress the balance.

5. Within any season, the same erratic behaviour is possible from place to place and from month to month: a poor start could be put right by a major dump; or weeks of sunshine could ablate a reasonable base.

6. However, if the season is preceded by a cold, snowy autumn which puts down a really good base, the chances are high that there will be adequate snow on the upper slopes throughout the season.

LIFE IN THE GREENHOUSE

In spite of reassurances, the concern about global warming during the 1980s (*see* Fig 6.1) cast a pall over the skiing fraternity in Europe. Combined with the fact that this was reinforced by a series of poor starts to the skiing season (*see* Fig 6.3a), an assumption was made that skiing's days were numbered and that Christmas winter-sporting holidays in the Alps were a thing of the past. In addition, it was widely accepted at the time that the solution was to head to the Rockies. The better snow in recent years in the Alps has, however, done something to calm the panic, but nevertheless there is still a suspicion that things have changed for good – in

spite of evidence of past records. It is therefore as well to look a little more closely at recent seasons both in the Alps and elsewhere to see whether the guide-lines set out above hold good under closer inspection, and if so what this means in terms of how to make decisions on when and where to go.

Recent Statistics

The analyses of snow conditions for the winter half of each year since 1980/1 for various regions in the northern hemisphere are set out in Table 6.1. It confirms much of what was said in the previous section and underscores the extent to which the variability within a given season can make so many holiday plans a lottery. Clearly, in the Alps between 1984/5 and 1989/90, the majority of seasons got off to a bad start, but it was only in the worst year (1988/9), which started relatively well before experiencing an extraordinary two months of unbroken dry, sunny weather, that the season never recovered. For the rest, the poor starts were more than compensated by good late-season snow which extended well beyond Easter.

An additional uncertainty is the variation that can be found across the Alps. In the worst seasons hardly anywhere escaped the dearth of snow, but subtle features in the weather patterns often resulted in significant differences from place to place. So, while the French Alps generally tended to be better in the dry years (*see* page 42), in 1988/9 the Arlberg, Oetztal and Dolomites did better. Generally, Italian resorts can fare well enough in good years. In bad years these resorts, in particular those in the Dolomites, tend to fare worst, although occasionally, as in 1984/85, the southern flanks come up trumps. It is therefore no wonder that the Sella Ronda was in the vanguard of installing snow-making machines during the 1980s.

A comparison of the snow conditions in the high level resorts in the Alps, Rockies and West Coast of North America, ranging from ★ (well below average) to ★★★★★ (well above average).

Year	Season	Alps	Rockies	West Coast
1980/1	Early	★★★★	★	★
	High	★★★★★	★	★
	Late	★★★★	★★★	★★★
1981/2	Early	★★★★★	★★★★	★★★★
	High	★★★★	★★★★★	★★★
	Late	★★★★	★★★★	★★★
1982/3	Early	★	★★★	★★★★★
	High	★★★	★★	★★★★★
	Late	★★★★	★★★	★★★★★
1983/4	Early	★★	★★★	★★★★
	High	★★★	★★	★★★
	Late	★★★★★	★★★★★	★★★★
1984/5	Early	★	★★	★★
	High	★★★★	★★	★
	Late	★★★	★★★	★★★
1985/86	Early	★★	★★★	★★★
	High	★★★★	★★	★★★★
	Late	★★★★★	★★★	★★★
1986/7	Early	★★★★	★	★★★
	High	★★	★★★	★★★
	Late	★★★	★★★★	★★★
1987/8	Early	★	★★★★	★★★
	High	★★★	★★★★	★★★★
	Late	★★★★★	★★★★	★★★★
1988/89	Early	★★★	★★	★★
	High	★	★★	★★
	Late	★★	★★★★	★★★★
1989/90	Early	★	★★★★	★★★★
	High	★★	★★	★★★
	Late	★★★★	★★	★★★
1990/1	Early	★★★	★★★★	★★★★
	High	★★	★★	★★★
	Late	★★	★★★★	★★★★
1991/2	Early	★★★★	★★	★★★
	High	★★	★★★	★★★
	Late	★★★★	★★★★	★★★
1992/3	Early	★★★★★	★★★★★	★★★★
	High	★★★	★★★★	★★★
	Late	★★★★★	★★★★	★★★
1993/4	Early	★★★	★★★★	★★
	High	★★★★	★★★	★★
	Late	★★★	★★	★★★

Table 6.1

The same story emerges when looking further afield. Although it is more difficult to draw simple conclusions when covering such a vast area as western North America, the same variations occur from year to year, within a season, and from place to place. In extreme cases, such as the 1980/1 season, the whole region experienced a drought of similar proportions to those that afflicted the Alps in the late 1980s. Over all, the advantages of the snowier areas (*see* page 51) do, however, stand out: in the Sierra Nevada, the Cascades, the coastal range of British Columbia and the Canadian Rockies, the snow records were generally more reliable. The same applies to the Utah resorts, while the figures in Colorado and New Mexico are more variable.

All of this, when combined with the data from other parts of the world, reinforces the basic rule that, if you are looking for reliable snow, there is no substitute for going to a high-altitude resort in a region that has high snowfall. Beyond this, the guide-lines identified in the previous section remain valid, but to them must be added the additional uncertainty that from year to year subtle shifts in large-scale weather patterns (*see* page 35) can make an appreciable difference to which resorts do best at any given time. Therefore, combining the snow reports with an ability to read the current weather situation and to interpret any forecasts can make a real difference in terms of choosing where to go.

LONG- AND SHORT-RANGE FORECASTS

When planning a winter holiday in the mountains, the ideal forecast would predict what the weather was going to be like during the season, when and how much snow was going to fall, and when long sunny periods could be expected. The drawback of such forecasts – if they were accurate – would be that everyone would want to take their holidays at the same time, this perhaps reducing enjoyment rather than improving it. In practice, however, such forecasts will never be available, so there remains a strong element of chance in all our plans. What we are concerned about here is trying to detect whether the meteorological dice is loaded.

Long-Range Forecasts

Starting with the longest forecasts, we have to accept that there are no well-defined cycles, so there is no point in working on the basis that every two, three, four or more years there will be a particularly good or bad season. More intriguing is whether there are signs in the run-up to any winter which indicate the seasonal weather to come. Everything from sunspots to the sea-surface temperatures of the tropical Pacific and how deep marmots are hibernating have been cited as useful guide-lines for forecasting weather. Analysis of these and other claims show that, with the exception of the behaviour of the tropical Pacific, there is little reason to put any faith in forecasts based on these indicators. Countless sophisticated studies have drawn an almost complete blank on reliable links between the eleven-year sunspot cycle and the Earth's weather, while, at the other extreme, behaviour of wildlife and the amount of berries on the trees tells us what the spring, summer and autumn weather has been like, not what form the succeeding winter will take.

The behaviour of the tropical Pacific is different in that there are good physical reasons why changes in this region can alter the weather around the world. Roughly every three to five years, a huge area of the equatorial Pacific warms up. This alters the amount of heat that is pumped into what might be called the 'boiler house' of the global weather engine, and so modifies global weather patterns. This phenomenon was first observed by Peruvian fishermen and, as it usually started around Christmas, was called El Niño (Spanish for 'boy child') because of the connection with the Nativity.

These changes in the sea-surface temperature and associated shifts in atmospheric-pressure patterns cause well-established areas of drought and floods throughout the tropics. However, more interesting in terms of mountain weather are the changes that occur in winter precipitation; these are most marked around the Pacific Rim, but there is a weaker signal further afield. Measurements of ice cores taken from glaciers from Mount Logan in the Yukon to Quilccaya in Peru show that snowfall at high levels increases during El Niño events all down the Western Cordillera of the Americas. A similar, but much less pronounced variation in precipitation can also be detected in Europe.

These effects can be detected in the data presented in Table 6.1. The El Niño years were 1982/3, 1986/7 and 1991–4. Conversely, the years when the tropical Pacific was cooler than normal were 1980/1, 1984/5 and, in particular, 1988/9. The fluctuations in snowfall recorded in the table do not tally precisely with the coming and going of the El Niño, but the correlation is high in western North America and New Zealand (not shown in Table 6.1) in particular, and even in the Rockies and the Alps there is a fair degree of agreement.

The reason why these connections are of interest to skiers is that following the most intense El Niño this century (1982/3), a huge amount of work was carried out to predict how and when these events occur. Computer models can now do a reasonable job of predicting the development of events six to nine months ahead, so it is possible to get a reason-able fix on whether an El Niño will occur, and how long and strong the event will be. Moreover, given the intense interest in the meteorological community these forecasts get wide publicity and so can be used to guide planning for winter holidays. However, while these developments do give a glimmer of hope that forecasts can be made as to the probability of a good or poor snow season in the coming winter, they say nothing about fluctuations within the season. This is a major limitation, because it is the variations from week to week that really matter.

Short-Range Forecasts

When it comes down to forecasts a week or two in advance, we move into a different domain. This is the world of numerical models that involve trillions of calculations on the largest super-computers. The products of this effort can be seen on our television screens every day and, contrary to popular belief, these short-term forecasts have improved substantially in recent years. They do, however, still have their limits, not least of which is that they currently only produce useful forecasts about five or six days ahead. Furthermore, theoretical studies of the potential for improvement suggest that however big the computer and however precise the measurements of the current state of the atmosphere, it will never be possible to produce useful predictions of the daily sequences of the weather more than about ten days in advance. Beyond that, all we can hope for are better analyses of the probabilities of temperature and precipitation variations.

What this means is that the best the forecasts can do is give us a pretty good idea what the weather is going to be like for the next few days, although even then the reliability of the forecasts varies with the weather conditions. Increasingly, forecasters are discovering that there are times when the weather is in a more predictable state and times when its behaviour is more erratic. When combined with the capacity of the mountains to generate their own weather in effect, even the standard forecasts may be of limited value.

There are, however, a few useful pointers. If the forecasters are confident in their predictions that a large high-pressure area is set to sit over the mountains for the coming week, then the chances are you will get a fine, dry week. However, if a series of depressions and associated fronts is predicted to sweep in from, say, the Atlantic or the Pacific, then even if the broad sweep of the forecast is right the precise timing and duration of adjacent stormy and clear spells is almost impossible to predict even a day or two in advance. In such unpredictable circumstances it is more important to be able to combine the standard forecasts with interpretations of the local weather conditions; in terms of making the most of your time in the mountains, this ability counts for a great deal.

READING THE SIGNS

Once in the mountains, many people's interest in the weather is transformed from something that is no more than a vague awareness to a central preoccupation. One target of this interest is to seek out local knowledge, and when this takes the form of mountain guides or ski instructors it can be an invaluable source of information. Too often, however, people rely on grizzled sages or simply rumour. Such predictions range from the psychotherapeutic, in the form of kindly locals assuring those desperate for new snow that their wish will be fulfilled that very night, to apocryphal observations that there will be no snow from Christmas until the end of January, when there will be a dump of

heroic proportions. The provision of such advice is part of local folklore, but it does not provide any real insight into the weather. On the other hand, the day-to-day signs that inform mountain guides are there for all to see, and with a little practice they can be read by anyone.

The starting point is to study the standard models of weather systems presented in Chapter 4, such as mid-latitude depressions and anticyclones. In practice, individual weather systems differ slightly from one another and, furthermore, their interaction with the mountains complicates matters. None the less, the underlying features are well known and, if care is used, developing weather events can be detected in good time. Moreover, if your observations are combined with the information provided by an up-to-date weather map or, better still, recent satellite imagery as shown on the television, you can become quite expert at your forecasting.

Anticyclones

The easiest situation to recognize is when a large static anticyclone sits over the mountains (*see* Fig 4.4). Apart from fog and low cloud down in the valleys (*see* Fig 6.8), this will give crisp, sunny weather with frost at night and, depending on the time of year, relatively warm to positively hot conditions by midday. The only real concern is to try to ascertain whether, and if so when, these conditions will break down. This will occur when the mobile depressions which run around the edge of such high-pressure areas start to encroach on the anticyclone. These depressions are guided by winds at altitudes of roughly 5–10km (16,400–32,800ft) – *see* page 35 – and so the obvious sign of when the anticyclone is in decline is when any high-level clouds start to move more quickly. Aircraft contrails provide excellent markers of

Fig 6.8 *Clouds in the valley. Sometimes the best sunshine is found high up in the mountains when there is low-altitude cloud. (Photograph by Rob Reichenfeld)*

these winds: when they stand stock still, it is a sure sign that the weather will not change rapidly; if, however, they fizz across the sky on what is otherwise a glorious day, then the chances are that the morrow will be less fine.

Fronts

Advancing weather fronts often produce warning clouds well ahead of their arrival. A classic sign of this is the formation of lenticular clouds on the tops of the highest mountains (*see* Fig 6.9); if combined with forecasts of a warm front moving into the area, they provide clear evidence of the movement of the approaching weather system. Since forecasting the exact progress of these fronts is

difficult, the use of on-the-spot observations to decide whether the weather is deteriorating more rapidly than expected can make all the difference between getting to safety in good time or being caught out in adverse conditions. During the winter of 1993/4, walkers and climbers stranded in the Highlands of Scotland complained that the blizzard conditions had arrived quicker than predicted. While they may have had some reason to grumble about the precision of the forecasts, the signs of impending storms were there to see hours before the bad weather actually struck. The ability to anticipate rapidly advancing weather systems is therefore an invaluable skill, especially if you are a long way from shelter.

Fig 6.9   *Lenticular altocumulus near the summit of the east face of Mount Cook (extreme left) in New Zealand on 26 January 1984. Mount Elie de Beaumont (right centre) and the head of Tasman Glacier (extreme right) are clearly visible. (Photograph by Richard Howes.)*

Although advancing warm fronts give good warning of their arrival, their departure may be more difficult to interpret. Not only may such warm fronts merge with their trailing cold fronts, but their own extent may also be blurred. Nevertheless, in unsettled periods of weather when the fronts are clattering through in close succession and skiing is at a premium, there may be brief breaks when the clouds remain at a low level but the sky is clear at the top of the mountains. In such circumstances, the sun may nearly break through lower down and, if the lifts are open, it pays to get to the highest levels possible. Here, you may ski on new snow above the clouds for an hour or two before the ensuing cold front brings a return of cloud and snow. During periods of bad weather such brief interludes of bliss wrested from the gloom are the source of intense satisfaction. Such stolen moments of pleasure should only be sought on pistes that are officially open, as it is folly to venture further afield in such unsettled conditions.

Cold fronts can creep up on you with less warning than warm fronts because they send out no outriding high clouds. However, if you know that a front is forecast to move in from a given direction, then the signs of its arrival will still be clear to see some time in advance. Furthermore, the more vigorous the front, the more marked will be the towering convective clouds which form its leading edge (*see* Fig 4.2). With the benefit of a prominent position high in the mountains, it should not be possible for such dramatic weather features to sneak up on you unawares, and to be caught out by such well-defined systems could be regarded as tantamount to negligence.

Local Developments

Of course, much of the time the weather in the mountains is not so clearly defined – clouds may drift up the valleys unexpectedly, or cumulus may develop swiftly over the peaks in warmer months. The significance of these local developments is usually difficult to interpret.

The most easily explained phenomena are the fair-weather cumulus that form around peaks on warm spring afternoons (*see* Fig 6.10), these being a sign that the hot sunshine on the bare ground down in the valley is causing warm air to rise upwards. These clouds usually represent no threat to skiers, climbers or walkers, but anyone venturing into the air with a hang-glider or parapente should take great care. Since a single-man parapente descends at around 400m (1,300ft) a minute, an updraught of 10m (30ft) per

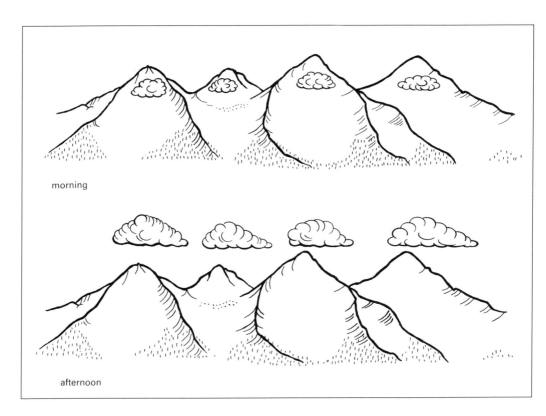

morning

afternoon

Fig 6.10   *How fairweather cumulus develop in spring. The valley floor warms up and air rises up the slopes to form clouds at lower levels in the morning; these then rise to sit over the peaks of the mountains in the afternoon.*

second will more than cancel this out and lift the parachute rapidly, thereby posing a major challenge to the pilot. Even more relevant is the localized nature of the heating effects. The strongest updraughts will be close to the mountain slope where the ground is heated, but near by there must be compensating downdraughts. These sudden shifts in vertical winds make parapenting even more hazardous and exciting as the mountains warm up in the spring. So, what look like innocuous clouds may in fact be clear evidence of strong thermals which need to be handled with care.

In more unstable conditions, when the air at higher levels is particularly cold, surface heating can generate convective cells which grow quickly into intense storms with thunder, lightning, squally winds and driving rain, hail and snow. In the Alps these conditions are common when a strong northwesterly or northerly flow covers western Europe. Often, such showery weather will coalesce into longer periods of continuous snow, and may generate a new depression in the lee of the mountains. However, even during clearer spells the prospect of showers is rarely far away, especially in March and April (*see* Fig 6.11).

White-out

Underlying all these observations is the problem of loss of visibility (*see also* page 23). The disorientating effect of going suddenly from bright, sunny weather into fog and cloud cannot be underestimated. Skiers know only too well that, even without being enveloped in fog, the flat light that comes with thick cloud overhead can make it impossible to see the bumps and difficult on gentle slopes to sense the direction of the gradient. On well-marked pistes these conditions can make the going confusing but manageable, but off piste it becomes far more demanding. The ability to navigate accurately in conditions of poor visibility is therefore essential.

When conditions deteriorate badly, visibility decreases further as the winds strengthen and drive the snow. The risk of going astray is even greater if you have to negotiate features such as cols, where funnelled winds are much stronger. It is therefore vital to recognize when conditions are about to go off and, if you cannot reach safety, to decide when it is too risky to go on and instead take shelter in a hollow or snow hole.

The course of action for piste skiers in such conditions is simple: it is better to stay below the tree-line on well-marked pistes where it is much easier to keep one's bearings. At higher levels it is possible to enjoy good skiing if there are adequate markings on pistes, and it is often easier to ski the steeper, bumpier slopes than to manage flatter, featureless areas. Once away from the marked runs, knowledge of the terrain is essential whether you are a skier or a walker. Failure to appreciate the consequences of blundering about in thick cloud or driving snow is pure folly. To conclude, all of this emphasizes the importance of having as much information as possible about current and impending weather conditions.

ACCESS TO WEATHER FORECASTS

There is now such detailed weather forecasting available in newspapers, on television or through fax, that ignorance of the weather is no excuse for being caught out. These forecasts provide a clear indication of what the general weather situation will be like for the coming few days. Television forecasts, especially those given on the weather channels in the United States, are particularly useful as they often include satellite pictures which

Fig 6.11 *A cold northerly outburst in spring brings showery weather to northern Europe and more prolonged snow to the northern slopes of the Alps and the Pyrenees. The snow-covered mountains of southern Norway also stand out spectacularly. This weather-satellite image was taken on 8 April 1980. (Reproduced with permission of the University of Dundee.)*

give a great deal of information about the current weather situation (*see* Fig 6.11). Being able to see the locations of the major weather systems can help in interpreting subsequent developments.

Such readily available forecasts are usually

sufficient for the needs of those who stick to the pistes or who take relatively short walks, but those who venture further afield should use more specialist information. Many national weather services around the world provide detailed forecasts for their mountain regions. Because these facilities are so extensive and designed for a variety of needs they are not listed here – it is better to find out about them when you go to the mountains. In the hands of guides and instructors, who can be expected to use such services, these forecasts offer a combination of wider analysis and local understanding. Whether you hire a guide or simply seek advice from such services, it pays to discover what forecasts are available and precisely what they mean for any planned expedition. It follows that the more you are able to interpret these forecasts, the greater will be the value of the local knowledge imparted by such consultation. It is vital, however, that you do not lose sight of the uncertainty in all these predictions – remember that it is not just yourself and your colleagues who may be at risk, but the rescue services that have to come to your aid in adversity.

7
Comfort and Safety

Here Skugg
Lies snug
As a bug
In a rug.
Benjamin Franklin (1706–90)

The extremes of mountain weather pose a challenge to us all. To enjoy activities in comfort in the face of such variety, we need to be able to respond flexibly to changing weather conditions. The range of temperatures skiers may experience – from sharp frosts and shady conditions to hot sunshine and temperatures as high as 20°C (68°F) on a spring day, and from sustained, biting daytime temperatures below −20°C (−4°F) to wet, humid, snowy conditions close to freezing, all within the space of a few days – places huge demands on clothing. Moreover, for many of us it is just as unpleasant being too hot as being too cold. It is therefore an essential part of activity planning to know what combination of equipment provides comfort and to have this to hand. To do this, it helps to know a little about the body's physiological responses to changing weather conditions.

THERMOREGULATION OF THE BODY

If we are to stay comfortable we need to take account of a number of processes. The first is the natural metabolic heat production of the body. Typically, this is around 100W when we are sitting still, and rises to around 350W when walking briskly and to 1,300W when climbing stairs. So, when climbing uphill, whether on foot or on skis, we generate heat at a rapid rate. Moreover, the main centres of heat generation shift from the trunk and the head to the muscles of the arms, legs and shoulders. When combined with the range of weather conditions that may occur, this increase and shift in heat production means that flexible clothing is essential if you are to remain comfortable. Sometimes, however, this is a major challenge. I find that skiing a steep mogul field during heavy, wet snowfall is akin to taking a Turkish bath. A decent skisuit keeps me dry but does not allow me to lose heat fast enough, but if I unzip the suit to the midriff I only end up getting drenched as melting snow collects inside it. It is a dilemma to which I have no solution. Fortunately, these conditions are rare, and for the most part modern clothing does provide the required flexibility. We do, however, still need to know a little about how the body loses heat and what different clothing can do to meet our personal needs if we are to be properly equipped.

76

Heat Loss

Normally we lose heat through a combination of conduction, convection, evaporation and radiation. Taking these processes in turn, conduction is simply the process whereby the air adjacent to the skin is heated. Convection is the associated loss of heat when the air is moving; in still air this process is driven by conduction of the body's heat, which causes warmed air to rise and be replaced by cooler air. In most cases, however, it is the fact that the air is moving which defines how important this process is. At low temperatures and high wind-speeds it can become the dominant factor. The measurement of this type of cooling and its physical consequences are discussed below.

Evaporation relies on the fact that conversion of water into vapour requires a lot of energy. By perspiring, the body can therefore control the amount of heat lost to the atmosphere. In normal circumstances, this process is only of importance at air temperatures above 20°C (68°F), when the combination of heat and humidity makes perspiring the principal means of keeping cool. This is rarely the case in the mountains in winter, where it is more usual that overheating is a result of being wrapped up too warmly. In such circumstances it is far more pleasant to remove excess clothing than rely on evaporative cooling, when rapid chilling can be uncomfortable at the low temperatures.

The combination of convection and evaporation is particularly important when inhaling and exhaling very cold, dry air. This can amount to 20 per cent of the body's total heat loss. This is important for mountaineers and ski-tourers who, when working hard, may lose large amounts of energy in this way and run the risk of a rapid drop in body temperature or even damage to their lungs.

Radiation effects are even more complicated. This process relies on the fact that all objects radiate heat at a rate related to their temperature. In the mountains, where the body is surrounded by cold surfaces, heat is radiated to these surroundings far more rapidly than the body receives heat from them. However, the heat from the sun can more than reverse the natural cooling effects, so the balance of cooling and heating due to radiation depends both on the weather and whether you are in sun or shade. This makes getting the right combination of clothing even more difficult.

WIND CHILL

The dominant impact of convective cooling in the form of wind chill requires separate consideration. In Britain this concept has only become popular in recent years, and as such it is the subject of a number of misconceptions. To some it is seen as an accurate definition of actual temperature, while to others it is seen as nothing more than a fad that has been imported from across the Atlantic along with so many other fashions. In fact, neither view is correct. Anyone who has lived in North America will know that exposure to the combination of intense cold and high winds that prevail when sudden cold waves sweep down across the eastern half of the continent cannot be reflected accurately by the temperature alone. The real physiological consequences of exposure to such conditions need to be understood if we are to respond effectively to the combined effects of wind and cold.

The first thing to get straight is that wind chill relates to *exposed* flesh. Early experiments to determine the rate of cooling from the skin were carried out in Antarctica by measuring the loss of heat from plastic cylinders full of warm water as a function of wind-

Wind Chill Equivalent Temperature as a Function of Wind-Speed and Air Temperature

		Wind-speed (km/h)					
		≤6*	10	20	40	60	80
Temperature (°C)	4	4	0	−5	−11	−13	−14
	0	0	−4	−10	−17	−19	−21
	−4	−4	−8	−15	−23	−26	−27
	−8	−8	−13	−21	−29	−32	−34
	−12	−12	−17	−26	−35	−39	−40
	−16	−16	−22	−31	−41	−45	−47
	−20	−20	−26	−36	−47	−51	−53
	−24	−24	−31	−42	−53	−58	−60
	−28	−28	−35	−47	−59	−64	−66
	−32	−32	−40	−52	−65	−70	−73
	−36	−36	−44	−57	−71	−77	−79

*Note   Still conditions are defined as wind-speeds less than 6km/h (4mph), equivalent to walking when there is no wind.

Table 7.1

speed. These experiments were designed to estimate the risks of frost-bite, but while the measurements taken and subsequent studies have provided a reasonable measure of loss of heat from the skin (*see* Table 7.1), this is all they can tell us. When wearing windproof well-insulated clothing, the only parts of the body experiencing the lower equivalent temperatures will normally be the exposed parts of the face. For the rest of the body, the heat loss is little different from that experienced in still conditions. Therefore, if the temperature is around freezing point, then it is easy to be too well wrapped up as modern clothing can provide a very high level of heat retention and windproofing.

A second and related point is that the wind-chill figures can be particularly misleading for temperatures above freezing. While the combination of 4°C (41°F) and a 40km/h (31mph) wind may feel like −11°C (12°F) on one's exposed flesh, there is no question that any freezing takes place in these conditions. In fact, the snow around you will be soft and thawing rapidly. In such circumstances, wind chill is even more dangerous in that it disguises the fact that the risk of avalanche is rising rapidly with the thaw. Remember, therefore, that wind chill is a useful guide to the consequences of getting caught out with inadequate protection rather than an absolute measure of the meteorological conditions. The most important message is that whenever venturing into the mountains, when wintry conditions can strike, at the very minimum have on you a complete set of windproof clothing.

All this highlights the value of understanding the climatology of any particular area. Where wind is a dominant factor, the temperatures often do not fall to very low values – in the Cairngorms at high levels the temperature rarely falls below −15°C (5°F), although in calm, cold conditions in sheltered upland valleys, night-time temperatures can fall much lower. This means that walkers, skiers or climbers in these areas need light, efficient windproofing. Kitting yourself up with gear that is designed to insulate against temperatures below −20°C (−4°F) will produce entirely the wrong effects when the temperature is, say, −4°C (25°F) and the wind-speed is 30km/h (19mph), for although the equivalent wind-chill temperature is −20°C (−4°F), the effect will be to overheat rapidly. Even if breathing fabrics are used in these conditions, there is a risk that you will become far too hot and sweaty, leading to personal discomfort and making a mess of expensive kit; worse still, if your clothes become sopping wet they will lose their insulating properties rapidly.

Conversely, where very low temperatures are likely to occur, as in the northern Rockies, Norway or in the Alps during the coldest spells, adequate insulation is paramount. At temperatures below −20°C (−4°F), even when the air is still, the rate of heat loss from poorly insulated clothing is rapid. Inadequate gloves, ill-fitting boots, or lack of warm head gear will soon result in extreme discomfort.

To conclude, for many winter activities we need to give careful thought not only to keeping warm but also to not getting uncomfortably hot. In order to understand how to achieve this happy combination, it pays to know a bit about how modern clothing both weatherproofs and insulates.

CLOTHING

Only fair-weather skiers who venture out on the balmiest of sunny days can ignore protection against the elements; anyone intending to get maximum enjoyment out of a standard holiday must give careful thought to what they need. For those walking, climbing or skiing far from shelter or the lift system, adequate protection is vital.

The type of protection needed depends both on the weather that you are likely to encounter and your physique. If you are built like a tank and break into a sweat at the merest provocation, your needs will be very different from those of wraith-like creatures who only get hot and bothered on blazing April days and who are liable to complain about the cold whenever it falls much below freezing. Whatever your metabolism, you will need the right combination of the following factors.

1. **Insulation**. Any clothing traps body warmth. Modern insulating materials provide the right combination of lightness and good thermal properties – typically, only 10–20 per cent of their volume is composed of fibre, the remainder being air. Goose or duck down is as good or better an insulator than modern materials, but is more susceptible to wetting (which reduces its insulating performance dramatically) and takes much longer to dry out. It is therefore possible to buy light and exceedingly efficient if somewhat bulky garments – often termed 'duvet' jackets and trousers – which can protect against the lowest temperatures. The performance of such garments is enhanced by using breathable reflecting linings, which trap the heat radiated by the body.

2. **Wind resistance**. As is evident from the previous discussion on wind chill, it is essential that clothes do not let the wind through; not only would this lead to wind chill, but it would also destroy the insulating properties of the garment as these rely on the air spaces between the fibres to produce efficient insulation. Modern, high-quality fabrics are vir-

tually 100 per cent windproof. Old-fashioned neoprene anoraks and plastic sheeting are also windproof, but these do not breathe, which is a serious drawback (see below).

3. **Waterproofing**. The outer fabric of any garment must not let in water and also must resist being wetted by it, otherwise it will become saturated. Again, high-quality modern materials can hold water under considerable hydrostatic pressure and have almost total repellency to wetting. Moreover, they largely retain their water repellence even after several washes.

4. **Breathability**. On average, the human body loses over 0.5 litres (1pt) of water in the form of perspiration per day, so it is essential to have clothing that allows this moisture to escape. The alternative is that it condenses inside the clothing, which both reduces the efficiency of insulation and is most uncomfortable when the wearer becomes chilled. The answer lies in fabrics such as Goretex, which contains an array of micropores that prevent droplets from penetrating from the outside but that are permeable to escaping water vapour. While Goretex is still regarded by many as the market leader, there are now several 'ultrabreathable' fabrics available that are capable of transmitting all the water vapour produced by the body in normal circumstances.

5. **Wicking**. Although breathable fabrics can handle normal rates of perspiration, they need assistance to deal with sweating brought on by heavy exercise, which can produce over 0.5 litres (1pt) per hour. In these circumstances, it helps if your underclothes and the linings of your outer garments are made of materials that can carry the moisture away from the body – for example, Sorel. Not only do these materials feel comfortable, but they also allow the breathable outer layers of your clothing to let the vapour escape. Various forms of thermal underwear combine high insulation with low absorption of moisture; this enables sweat to evaporate away from the body, thereby increasing the chances of the skin staying warm and dry.

Clearly, combining this range of material properties with both your personal requirements and the range of weather conditions you are likely to experience provides a range of options. It is therefore as well to establish a set of priorities. First and foremost, it is essential that your clothing is sufficiently windproof and waterproof to protect you from any sudden deterioration in the weather. Without this you run the risk of getting cold and wet which, if you are far from shelter, is both perilous and foolhardy. This means that you must at least have a decent lightweight weatherproof anorak and trousers, beneath which you can wear what you like.

Second, for comfort your clothing should be sufficiently adaptable so that you keep warm, but at the same time do not overheat during the normal range of conditions you might expect during any given day. All-in-one garments do not stand up well on this count for, although they may keep you wonderfully snug in a blizzard, they give you a torrid time when you are working hard in the noonday sun, even though the temperature may be well below freezing. Furthermore, such garments can reduce your mobility if they are too bulky. Instead, it is better to have a combination of lightweight, thermally efficient clothes and a breathable, waterproof and windproof outer jacket and trousers. Not only do the layers trap additional air and hence improve the insulation, but you can add and subtract layers to respond to the changing conditions. These adjustments can be made both in response to the weather forecast and also during the day if you carry a small rucksack for reserve clothing.

The same approach applies to protecting the extremities. The hands need particular attention, for not only are frozen fingers exceedingly painful but they also make it difficult to adjust equipment. Mittens reduce heat loss, but modern gloves, when new, can provide very high levels of insulation. Wearing silk or thinsulate glove liners is an excellent way of getting additional protection, as well as removing the risk of your flesh sticking to any supercooled metal – a huge benefit if you are wearing mittens and need to adjust your equipment. The head is equally important as a great deal of heat is lost from here in very cold weather when you are well wrapped up. Any combination of caps, hats and headbands should therefore be used to control heat loss, and to protect the ears. In cold, sunny conditions, when a hat may not seem necessary, a light headband is the answer for anyone who has jughandle ears such as mine!

As for choosing clothes, it pays to do some research. Specialist manufacturers provide a lot of technical information about their clothing's performance, giving tog values, and water resistance, moisture permeability and water repellency figures. Leaving aside matters of style and fashion, the simple rule is that you get what you pay for. So, if you want high-performance, lightweight clothing which is easy to move around in, you will need to look to the specialist manufacturers to meet your needs. However, do remember to gear your decisions both to your own sensitivity to heat and cold, and the weather you are likely to meet. If you feel the cold and plan to ski in the Canadian Rockies in January and February, your requirements will be much more demanding than if you were planning to potter around Meribel at Easter.

AVALANCHE SAFETY

A great deal has been written about the detection and avoidance of avalanche risk and what to do during and following an avalanche (*see* Further Reading), so there is no need to go over this ground in detail. What is more relevant is to link how dangerous conditions develop in the snowpack with the safety information that is more widely available. In bringing out the essential meteorological aspects of this tricky subject, the aim will be to highlight the areas where there is reasonable agreement on what really matters. More important is to realize how much can be conveyed in a book and what can only be learnt on the spot, where local knowledge must be relied upon. This is an area where a little learning can be a dangerous thing, so it must be emphasized that what is presented here is not designed to be an instruction manual, but rather an attempt to provide some insight into the fascinating complexity of the subject.

Types of Avalanche

Avalanches fall into two broad categories: loose snow avalanches (*see* Fig 7.1) and slab avalanches (*see* Fig 7.2). The first occur in both wet and dry snow which has not consolidated. They gain in volume as they slide down the slope, so a small slide may eventually build up into a very large and dangerous avalanche. In contrast, slab avalanches start when an area of consolidated snow starts to move down the mountain. While these types of avalanche can trigger additional snow movements, the major impact is associated with the initial release of snowpack.

Both types of avalanche come in many forms and sizes. Loose snow avalanches can range from small slides of light powder, which are only a threat to mountaineers on

Fig 7.1 *A slope cleared by the effect of two loose-snow avalanches. (Photograph by E Wengi, reproduced with permission of the Institute of Snow and Avalanche Research, Weissfluhjoch.)*

the steepest slopes, to huge affairs that can result in tens of thousands of tonnes of new snow sweeping down the mountainside for as much as 2–3km (1–2 miles), and destroying everything in their path. The largest powder avalanches can generate wind-speeds over 300km/h (200mph), which can flatten trees beyond the run-out zone. Similarly, slab avalanches can range from limited slides of compacted snow to major slides which strip whole mountainsides and sweep away any trees and property in their path.

Avalanche Risk

It is obvious that the risk of avalanches will depend on the angle of the slope on which the snow collects, the depth of the snow and the condition of the snow. It is equally evident that, of these three factors, only the angle of the slope can be measured with any degree of accuracy. So, starting with the easy bit, avalanche statistics show that the most vulnerable slopes for slab avalanches are those between 35 and 40 degrees. Such avalanches rarely occur on slopes less than 20 degrees and greater than 50 degrees as the former are too flat and the latter are usually too steep to collect appreciable accumulations of snow. However, wet, melting snow may slide on even shallower slopes, and sloughs of new snow may occur on slopes steeper than 50 degrees when snowfall during calm conditions enables a temporary build-up to occur.

Fig 7.2   *A large slab avalanche clears entire mountain slopes on the Schwarzhorn near Davos. (Photograph by S Gliott, reproduced with permission of the Institute for Snow and Avalanche Research, Weissfluhjoch.)*

Just how complicated avalanche prediction has become is indicated by the claim that the risk is increasing in the Alps with the shift from agriculture to tourism. The decline in upland grazing in the summer means that the cows do not crop the grass so short. Longer grass is not only beaten down by the snow but may ferment slowly during the winter to provide a slippery surface. This combination makes it easier for snow to slide off in the spring.

As for the depth of snow and its state, the points made in Chapter 2 are encapsulated in Fig 7.3. This presentation gives a rough guide to how the risk of avalanches develops over time, and the processes summarized underlie the warnings that are prepared and provided by authorities around the world. Until recently, there was a rather complicated eight-level hierarchy of warnings for avalanches in the Alps. At the bottom, the rating of one indicated that the hazard was very slight, but recognized that in the mountains a hazard rating of zero did not exist. At the top, a level of eight warned of an exceptional avalanche situation when numerous avalanches were likely as a result of enormous accumulations, there being a high probability that large avalanches would cause major damage to property. The risk-measurement scale has now been reduced to levels one to five (*see* Table 7.2).

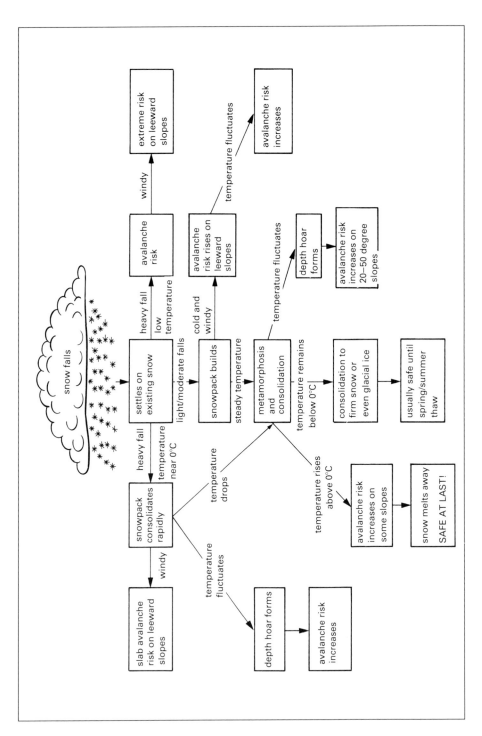

Fig 7.3 *Almost wherever you look in some parts of the mountains, various combinations of snowfall and temperature fluctuations can lead to avalanche risks, and the more it snows and the more the temperature varies, the greater the risk. This flow diagram aims to give some impression of how the continuous interaction between the weather and snow changes the risk,*

Avalanche Warning Levels

Level 1 Slight risk – zero risk does not exist. Slides of snow are only possible on rare, isolated, steep slopes, particularly when subjected to a heavy burden, such as that which a large group of skiers might create.

Level 2 Limited risk. Generally only on slopes that are clearly identified in the bulletins as being likely to have ill-stabilized snow conditions, and where the presence of skiers produces a heavy load on the snow.

Level 3 Marked risk. On sufficiently steep slopes there is a general risk that the presence of skiers will cause slides, and the spontaneous release of avalanches is very likely in some places.

Level 4 High risk. The snowpack is only weakly stable and the chance of avalanches is considerable with even the slightest disturbance on many slopes of most gradients; spontaneous slides are widespread.

Level 5 Very high risk. The snowpack is generally unstable, with numerous and large avalanches likely on most slopes, including terrain with only a slight gradient.

Table 7.2

There are several important features of the new system of warning levels. First, as is made clear in level one, there is never a zero risk of avalanches. Even when there has been no new snow for many days or even weeks, and temperatures have been reasonably steady, there may still be isolated places on steep slopes where the snow has become dangerously unstable. Second, the levels provide broad indications of the dangers and cannot be used to make assumptions about any particular slope. Although the avalanche services in many countries draw on large numbers of trained observers to reach decisions about the level of risk, the published figures can only be used as a guide. Climbers, skiers and walkers therefore have to combine these warnings with the conditions they encounter in the mountains. Not only does this underline the importance of relying on local expertise when venturing off the beaten track, but also of learning as much as you can about the places where danger may lurk (*see* Further Reading).

Looking for signs of how the weather will have contributed to dangerous conditions is the first step in improving one's knowledge. At the simplest level, this amounts to finding out from experts why warnings have been issued and what particular factor has changed. If there has been a heavy fall of snow the risk is obvious, but if changes in temperature have been the cause then it will pay to find out more about why these have led to heightened warnings. It may therefore be necessary to find out more about what the weather has been like in recent weeks or even months. Various combinations of snowfall, cold, dry spells or even thaws can be interpreted in terms of the flow diagram shown in Fig 7.3 to provide greater insight into why conditions have become more dangerous.

Once out on the slopes, there are plenty of signs to indicate where more dangerous conditions will occur. In particular, any indication of the prevailing wind direction is invaluable. The presence of a cornice (*see* Fig 7.4) is a sure sign of both the wind direction and also that deeper snow will be found in the lee of the slope (*see* Fig 2.9). Other indica-

85

Fig 7.4 *Formation of a cornice on the Mittel-grat. (Photograph by E Wengi, reproduced with permission of the Institute for Snow and Avalanche Research, Weissfluhjoch.)*

tions of the wind include, at the extreme edge of the tree-line, tattered and wind-torn trees whose branches point in the direction of the prevailing wind, a build-up of rime on the windward side of exposed obstacles, and tell-tale hollows in the lee of rocks that have been scooped out by the wind. Such signs tell us how the winds will sculpt the snow in a locality. Because these winds are a product of the local topography, the only way of recognizing their effects is to read these signs on the spot – knowledge of wider weather patterns serves no real purpose in this context.

Translating the meteorological evidence

into safe practice is a far greater challenge. Clearly, obvious cornice-capped leeward slopes, especially if they catch the noonday sun, should be given a wide berth. By comparison, windward slopes and exposed ridges, providing you steer well clear of overhanging cornices, offer safer routes. Beyond this, the more subtle features of how snow builds up and disguises the lie of the land can only be learnt as a result of lengthy experience.

Survival Rates

The widely quoted figures in both Europe and the United States for survival rates of people buried in avalanches show a monotonic decline with time (*see* Figs 7.5a and 7.5b). They suggest that while 80 per cent are alive after ten minutes, the figure declines to around 40 per cent after an hour and to only 20 per cent after two hours.

Recent research using data of all Swiss avalanche disasters from 1981 to 1991 produces a more complicated and pessimistic picture (*see* Fig 7.5c). Of the 422 buried skiers, 241 (57 per cent) were dead on extraction, and on average they were buried under about 1m (3ft) of snow. Initial survival rates were rather higher than the standard model, with only eight dead out of 123 skiers rescued within fifteen minutes. Furthermore, only two of these had been asphyxiated, the others having died from injuries sustained in the avalanche. More depressing is the fact that the survival rate plummets to only 30 per cent after thirty-five minutes. It then remains virtually steady until around ninety minutes, and then falls from a figure of 27 per cent to only 3 per cent surviving more than two hours.

The interpretation of the high mortality statistics between fifteen and thirty-five minutes suggests that anyone who is buried in an avalanche without an air pocket around

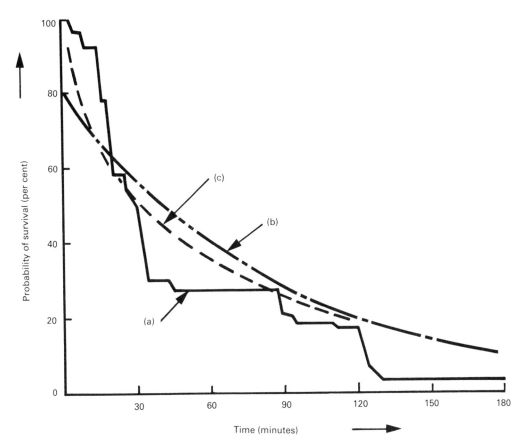

Fig 7.5 *Early rescue is vital. Recent statistics on the chances of survival in avalanches in Switzerland between 1981 and 1991 (a) present a different picture to earlier European (b) and United States statistics (c).*

their face will suffocate within about half an hour. Thereafter, survival depends on having a certain amount of air around the face. The additional survival time of about an hour to an hour and a half is related to both the amount of air in the pocket around a buried person's face and also how quickly they cool down. While hypothermia is an unlikely consequence of being trapped, given the benefits of sheltering in a snowhole if caught out on the mountains at night or in bad visibility (*see*

page 73), it is a killer if combined with a lack of air. The chances of survival beyond two hours are therefore awfully slim if you are buried deep in an avalanche.

This new data contains a set of vitally important messages for those skiing or touring off piste. First, since over two-thirds of those buried by avalanches will die within half an hour or so, their survival is critically dependent on being dug out by someone in the vicinity; the rescue services will not

87

necessarily get there in time. This grim statistic underlines how essential it is to observe the basic safety rules when crossing potentially unsafe slopes. In particular, if you are in a party the rigid requirement to cross these slopes *one at a time* cannot be overemphasized; your colleagues will be the only people who can dig you out in time. It also underlines the fact that, if you see anyone swept away by an avalanche, it is essential to concentrate fiercely on where they were last seen, because this may be a matter of life or death when it comes to digging them out quickly. In this respect, carrying a lightweight shovel in your rucksack is of immense value in moving snow quickly. The other sombre feature of the dependence on immediate action is that it explains the worrying fact that, in spite of much improved rescue services, the survival rates did not improve during the 1980s.

The second point is the value of creating an air pocket. Speaking personally, and having never been in such an awful predicament, I remain gravely suspicious of one's ability to take such evasive action when being swept away in a blinding wall of snow. But, if as seems the case, the creation of an air pocket around your head can more than triple your survival time, then covering your face with your hands and arms seems to be the number one priority. This is probably a better strategy than trying to 'swim' to the surface, given that even under 30cm (1ft) of snow you will be incapable of escape, and taking into account that the statistics indicate that only one in five people trapped by avalanches ended up with their heads this close to the surface.

8
Putting it all Together

We for a certainty are not the first
Have sat in taverns while the tempest hurled
Their hopeful plans to emptiness, and cursed
Whatever brute and blackguard made the world.
AE Housman (1859–1936)

In summing up how weather matters should be included in planning mountain activities, it is important to retain a sense of proportion. While the weather may be the dominant factor at certain points, it is only one element in getting real pleasure out of the mountains, and has to be ranked alongside the atmosphere and beauty of the location, the challenges you are looking for, and how much solitude you need. So, if you have decided that the only place to spend Christmas is St Moritz or that you want to complete the Haute Route in April, then the weather only comes into play in day-to-day planning. If, on the other hand, you are going to take a skiing holiday at short notice somewhere in North America or Europe, then knowing more about the weather and snow conditions can make all the difference.

SAFEST BETS

Starting with those who wish to book their holidays in advance and who have little flexibility in terms of timing, the climatological records provide some pretty clear messages. If, for example, you are limited to skiing during school holidays, the implications are pretty obvious. First and foremost, if you are looking for a combination of good snow, settled weather and plenty of sunshine, then the safest approach is to choose a big, high-level resort with a proven snow record. In the Alps, such a resort would be at a minimum of 1,500m (4,900ft) and would provide plenty of readily accessible skiing above about 2,000m (6,600ft). Suitable destinations include the better-known French resorts – for example, Val d'Isère, the Trois Vallées, La Plagne and Alpe-d'Huez – while elsewhere in the Alps, resorts such as Verbier, Zermatt, Ischgl/Galtür, Obergurgl and Obertauern would come high on the list. In North America, the choice of suitable resorts is greater, with those in Utah, above Lake Tahoe, at Blackcomb/Whistler and in the Canadian Rockies being in the vanguard.

When it comes to timing, the choice between Christmas, late February (when many schools have half-term holidays) and Easter is a balancing act. Clearly, Christmas is the riskiest time, for not only are the days short and the snow cover thin, but there is also a tendency for the weather in the mid-latitudes of the northern hemisphere to be more than usually unsettled at this time. Maximizing daylight hours and sunshine means going to southerly areas with good sunshine figures, such as Colorado. By comparison, late February is much safer, the snowpack at resort level normally being at its deepest and the days being pleasantly long. As for Easter (providing it does not fall too late in April), there should be plenty of snow at high levels and even longer days. The warmer days do, however, mean that snow at lower levels and on sunny slopes will be mushy from late morning, and so the amount of good skiing may be less than that found earlier in the season.

As noted in Chapter 5, changes in the weather are less significant in the Alps and for much of western North America throughout the winter and early spring, the conditions remaining variable. So there is no clear reason for choosing late February in preference to Easter (or vice versa) on the basis of getting better weather. However, in those areas where shifts in the major storm tracks exert a greater influence, such as Scotland, the chances of the weather improving in late March and April are considerable. Similarly, declining precipitation during March in California, combined with abundant sunshine and the product of the usually reliable heavy winter snowfall, make the resorts around Lake Tahoe just about the safest bet for excellent late-season skiing.

Type of Resort

The emphasis on big resorts is important as it increases the prospects of finding some slopes with good conditions. You should look for resorts which have slopes with different aspects and runs at varying altitude, a bonus especially in the coldest weather. Sheltered nursery slopes are also a must for beginners and children.

Resorts such as Kühtai, Obergurgl and Obertauern, with their limited altitude range,

can be awfully exposed when it is bitterly cold. The same is less true of the big French resorts, as the highest of these are usually connected to lower lying villages. This means that in late January it is often better to go to these villages rather than the likes of Val Thorens, Tignes or Belle Plagne. In high, cold resorts with good snow records the type of lifts can also make a lot of difference: long drag-lifts out of the sun and open, windy chair-lifts can test even the best clothing; by comparison, telecabins ('bubbles') and cable-cars provide much more protection. It is therefore worth finding out more about what types of lift are on offer in the different resorts (*see* Further Reading).

None of this rules out the lower Austrian resorts with their pretty villages and *Gemütlichkeit* or the fashionable watering-holes. All it means is that if you are intent on going to Gstaad, Kitzbühel, Mayrhofen or Megève early or late in the season, the risk of getting poor snow is high, and the chances are that you may have to queue not only to get up to the snow but also to get down again. In this respect, resorts such as Kitzbühel, which have been reluctant to put in snow-making equipment to increase the chances of getting back to the village on skis, cannot be surprised if their reputation has fallen as other resorts have proved more enterprising. Conversely, less well-endowed resorts that have put in extensive snow-making facilities, such as those in the Dolomites, do offer a greater chance of being able to ride out a bad patch. Therefore, it also pays to check if and how much snow-making is offered by resorts before booking.

Incidentally, don't be taken in by grizzled old ski instructors who tell you that there were never bad seasons in the 'good old days'. While it is true that the low-lying Austrian resorts were hit particularly hard at the end of the 1980s, it is not true that they never faced such shortages in the past. Any Kitz-bühler with a long and accurate memory will admit that 1957, 1964 and 1972 were all disastrous seasons, and if you really want to show off you could add that 1936 and 1922 were also pretty awful, as was 1897.

Even if you are intent on going somewhere with a certain type of ambience, it pays to exploit climatological information. As Chapter 5 makes clear, Fieberbrunn or Waidring offer more substantial snowfall than other low-lying Austrian resorts. Alternatively, you can go a little higher and still get a pretty village in, say, Alpbach. But, with the best will in the world, it is still very risky to plan a holiday in these resorts at Christmas or after early March: not only will the snow either have yet to arrive or be disappearing from the lower slopes, but in resorts that have nothing to offer above about 1,750–2,000m (5,700–6,500ft) there is little prospect of finding decent or extensive high-level skiing. Access to a separate glacier area (such as at Kaprun, Mayrhofen, Neustift or Zell am See), may prove to be more of a snare and delusion when the snow is poor lower down – the horrendous queues to get up and down will simply destroy all the fun.

SNOW REPORTS

If you have greater flexibility in when you can take holidays but are not willing to leave bookings to the last minute, then you will still have to rely largely on climatology. Depending on when you choose to book you may also be able to draw on information about early snow and, in particular, take heart from good autumnal snowfall. For the rest, the flexibility in timing enables you to miss the crowds and possibly find cheaper deals. In this context, skiing in mid- and late January offers good value. Although many people are scared off by the threat of cold weather at this time, it is balanced by the fact that even the lower resorts are likely to have decent snow which will not deteriorate rapidly even with unbroken sunshine. Even more rewarding can be a trip taken before Christmas or after Easter to the best-endowed high resorts, when the combination of low prices, deserted slopes and good snow is intoxicating.

If you are prepared to take a chance then it does pay to book late as you will be able to exploit up-to-date knowledge of the conditions. Such information is available in a variety of forms, including travel articles in newspapers, media stories on the weather and reports from friends. The best-known sources, however, are the snow reports published in the newspapers, on Ceefax or available on telephone hot-lines. These reports ran into a lot of criticism at the end of the 1980s when skiers in the Alps found that the reports had been 'economical with the truth' and had disguised some pretty dire conditions. Some well-publicized stories of supposedly good snow being no more than limited areas of rocky slush have ensured that the information now supplied has improved. None the less, it still pays to read between the lines.

Snow Depth

The most important statistic is the snow depth, and although the figure given will inevitably be an approximation, it has to bear some resemblance to reality. So, a resort reporting 50cm (20in) or more of snow on the lower slopes should be sporting a perfectly adequate base. However, when the figures for the lower slopes get down to around 10–20cm (4–8in), then be on your guard. Furthermore, if such niggardly figures are combined with comments describing the runs to the resort as either 'poor' or 'closed', then the nursery slopes are likely to be a mess, and you will want to use rented skis in order to get back to the village.

Temperature

The temperatures quoted in snow reports are of doubtful provenance, so do not attach too much importance to them, although when combined with the comments they can be of more value. If temperatures are below −10°C (14°F) and there are comments about excellent snow and bitter cold then they provide a useful picture. Equally, if temperatures are well above freezing and the comments describe rain, thawing or avalanche danger then you know the conditions are deteriorating rapidly. However, if the temperatures are well above freezing but the comments are all about good snow, then it may simply mean that the thermometer used by the reporter is catching the afternoon sun!

Recent Snowfall

The date of the most recent snowfall is illuminating, especially if you can find out how much fell at the time. The longer it has been since there was a decent fall, the greater the likelihood that the conditions will be going off. Many off-piste areas will develop a hard crust after a period without snow, but resorts with an adequate base will be able to keep the pistes in good order and, if the temperatures are low enough at night, will be able to make snow to improve the busiest runs. None the less, it is a big plus to know that there has been recent or substantial snowfall when deciding whether and where to go for a last-minute holiday.

Interpreting Comments

As already noted, the comments in the reports can be particularly useful. Where they are bubbling over with enthusiasm about the magnificent conditions there is no problem; it is the more guarded euphemisms that require interpretation. Comments such as 'sunny skiing on the glacier' probably means that the rest of the resort is in a poor state, and everyone there is trying to ski the few modest blue runs on offer. Furthermore, if there is no easy way down from the glacier, there will be horrendous queues not only to get up to the snow, but also down again.

Warning bells should also go off when you read comments such as 'reasonable skiing on the pistes that are open', or 'still good skiing to be found above 2,500m'. When such comments are combined with further observations to the effect that the runs to the resort are 'poor' and off-piste conditions are 'varied', it will be clear that there is not much on offer. What they are saying, in fact, is that any good runs will be swarming with people and the runs down will consist of icy ribbons of rock-strewn artificial snow which only experts could negotiate with ease – not that they would want to risk their own skis.

Resort Performance

Over the years the snow reports have also provided a useful check on the performance of the best-known resorts. This is helpful both in interpreting individual reports and in making choices. Not surprisingly, the big, high-altitude French resorts such as Val d'Isère, La Plagne and Val Thorens do well, as do St Anton and Obergurgl – although the latter tends to have less snow than other successful resorts, but hangs on to it best thanks to its height. Slightly more surprising is the remarkably good record of Flaine (within spitting distance of Geneva), which seems to benefit particularly from wringing most out of weather systems as they first hit the Alps (*see* page 27).

Conversely, there are notable disappointments. Leaving aside lower resorts, including the highly fashionable centres as mentioned earlier, Verbier tends to have less reliable snow cover at low levels than its competitors, in spite of doing well at high altitudes. Less surprising is the poor record of Wengen, where the combination of its relatively low altitude (1,240m, or 4,067ft) and vulnerability to the föhn (*see* page 39) reduce the prospects of reliable snow. The reports also confirm the earlier comments about the unreliable snow in the Dolomites. Finally, look carefully at the reports for the Trois Vallées. This massive ski area has a justifiably high reputation, but the runs down into Meribel, which are central to linking up the whole system, catch an awful lot of sun and deteriorate quickly – a feature that is sometimes revealed in the snow reports.

North American Resorts

The same general rules apply to resorts in North America, but given the wide spread of locations, there is more need to combine the reports with information about the general climatology of any specific resort. In particular, remember how cold the northern Rockies can be in January and February and how stormy the West Coast ranges are in midwinter. Also, be on your guard for spring warmth stripping the lower slopes in resorts which do not get a lot of snow at low levels. For instance, in spite of its generally excellent snow record, Jackson has a reputation for losing its cover early on its predominantly south-facing slopes. Furthermore, because the weather warms up here more rapidly than it does in the Alps, there may be less opportunity for topping up the runs back to the resort with artificial snow.

Europe and North America?

Leaving decisions until a late stage is particularly valuable in deciding whether to holiday in Europe or North America. As is clear from the long-term snow statistics, the arguments in favour of choosing, say, the Rockies in preference to the best in the Alps are not clear-cut; while there may be any number of reasons for making a particular choice, the snow records for North America do not stand head and shoulders above those of the Alps. Only if you are intent on finding some deep, light, powder snow does the case for going to Utah win hands down. Once the season is in progress, evidence that either Europe or western North America is having a poor season can be the deciding factor.

The same arguments apply to less sought-after destinations if resorts in both the Alps and the Rockies are generally having a poor season. For instance, if northern Europe is having a cold winter, the Italian Alps and the Dolomites may have better snow (*see* page 32); even so, take a belt-and-braces approach and choose a high resort such as Sestriere or Cervinia to be on the safe side. Alternatively, it is possible that the snow may be better in eastern Europe or Norway, or even in New England or Scotland. Also, while only very rarely, as at the beginning of the 1994/5 season, do the Pyrenees have better snow than the Alps, in good years they offer highly competitive options.

If resorts in the Rockies and California are having a bad season, it may be the ideal year to go to the Pacific North West. The fact that the Coast Ranges have so much snow means that even in drought years places such as Blackcomb/Whistler will, in all probability, have more than adequate snow; it is in the snowy years that they are likely to have too much of a good thing, with stormy, cloudy conditions prevailing.

In the best years most resorts in the Alps will offer decent snow. If this is the case then decisions on where to go can be made on the basis of factors other than snow conditions – especially in the low season, when an over-supply of accommodation means there should be plenty of genuine bargains to be had. Furthermore, the cheapness of resorts in Italy will more than compensate for any residual risk of getting slightly less good snow.

OTHER INTERESTS

So far this look at using weather information in the decision-making process has concentrated solely on the needs of skiers. There is, however, no reason why the same principles cannot be applied to other activities. For instance, family holidays may have to meet a variety of interests, covering not only down-hill skiing, but also walking and langlaufing. While the requirements of the downhillers tend to be more demanding in terms of snow, they may not adequately cover these other interests. As a general rule, these wide-ranging needs are better catered for in tradi-tional resorts rather than in the neo-brutalist concrete monstrosities that have been built above the tree-line to pander to the every need of downhillers – while vast swathes of reliable motorway skiing fit their bill, they do not make for scenic walking or langlaufing. So, places such as Wengen and Seefeld, which are so well equipped for other activities but also have a reasonable range of skiing, may offer a better compromise in spite of being more risky in terms of snow cover. If snow is what you really want then it may be better to go to Norway where the lower tem-peratures will improve the chances that your needs are met.

Once downhill skiing ceases to be of interest, then the scope of where to go widens dramatically; indeed, it becomes too wide to summarize the ways of choosing between all the options. Instead you must decide what you are looking for by way of outdoor activi-ties and how much these may be affected by the weather. If you conclude that your enjoy-ment will be marred by adverse conditions then it is valuable to consider how this risk can be minimized.

In the case of hillwalkers, these considera-tions are further extended by the fact that there are no restrictions to any particular time of the year. So, while nearly all skiers, save those who enjoy cavorting on glaciers, will have packed their equipment away, more resolute walkers in the Alps can still reach the high snows in summer. For this reason, the statistics given in the Appendix cover the whole year. What is evident from these figures is that at levels above about 2,500m (8,200ft) it can sometimes get very cold at night, and above this level in cool, cloudy spells of weather there is an even chance that it may snow rather than rain. Even in high summer, walkers venturing high into the Alps should therefore be equipped to fend off cold, squally weather.

Other mountain ranges offer such a huge range of different conditions outside winter that it is best to rely on the statistics to gain an inkling of what the weather will be like. An example of the more subtle differences is given by the Pyrenees which, although they are a slightly milder version of the Alps in the winter, are much drier at corresponding levels in summer. Consequently, they offer a combination of spectacular scenery and ideal weather conditions for high-mountain walk-ing in summer. No wonder enthusiasts hold the mountains in such high regard.

CONCLUSIONS

When all is said and done, there is only so much you can do about the weather. Having considered the extent to which the weather matters in your plans and taken appropriate action to reduce its adverse impact, you then have to live with your decisions. If you are lucky and achieve precisely what you wanted then the sense of satisfaction is immense. But, even if you have done all the right things in terms of choosing the time and place, ensuring that you are properly equipped and seeking local guidance on where to go to find the conditions you most earnestly desire, there is still every prospect that a bout of beastly weather will blow your hopeful plans to emptiness.

In these circumstances the only approach is to be both phlegmatic and realistic. If you have truly gone to considerable lengths to optimize your chances of success, then the only solution is to accept that these things happen and make the best of the situation. However, this does not mean that you can assume things are bound to change after a run of bad luck, and hence it is all right for you to take greater risks. Similarly, as time runs out on a holiday and the conditions steadfastly refuse to improve there is no point in trying to press ahead with a planned expedition come what may. Nothing is more dangerous than becoming frustrated by vile weather to the extent that you disregard all the safety rules; succumbing to this temptation is the ultimate folly.

If you are properly equipped and informed it is possible to make the most of bad weather. This is part and parcel of the advice contained in this book, for whatever the weather it is possible, by the application of relatively simple rules, to get a little more out of the conditions. The cumulative effect of these principles can add up to appreciable advantages in getting more of what you want, and the knowledge that making the right choice means scoring over those who get it wrong can be rewarding. Moreover, if this success results in reducing the risk of needlessly chancing one's arm then it is even more deeply satisfying. It is not a matter of removing all risk – this is simply not possible, for the uncertainties of mountain weather are ever-present – but a matter of taking full advantage of readily available information to reduce these risks to an acceptable level. If, like me, you are looking for a combination of sun, snow and mountains that makes your heart soar, I hope this book helps. Good hunting.

Appendix:
Facts and Figures

Means, monthly means, how shall we tell your meaning?
Sir Napier Shaw, *Drama of the Weather* (1933)

This appendix provides additional climatological information on mountain regions around the world. Where possible, the figures relate to places described in the text, but in many cases there is no reliable data for high altitudes. This means that in order to estimate roughly what conditions prevail in any particular place you will have to extrapolate from the figures for the nearest site provided here. The simple adjustment of reducing the mean monthly temperature ($T°C$) by 1°C for every increase of 150m (or 3.6°F for every 1,000ft) in altitude above the quoted sites will not lead you far astray. In the case of precipitation (p, in mm of rainfall or rainfall equivalent), the broad figures of doubling from sea-level to 1,500m (5,000ft) and by about a factor of 2.5 going from 1,500m (5,000ft) to 3,000m (10,000ft) given in Chapter 2, provide a useful guide to how much more will fall at higher levels. This rule of thumb should, however, be used with caution.

Where available, statistics are provided on hours of bright sunshine (S) and extreme temperatures. The latter come in two forms. In some cases they are given as the average high and low figures that can be expected in any given month (T_h and T_l). These are of more use to holidaymakers than the highest and lowest figures ever recorded at a given

site (T_H and T_L) as they provide a measure of the extremes we might normally experience in a week or two's holidaying. However, where monthly maxima have not been computed, and where record highs and lows are available, these extremes are provided to give some idea of the range of temperatures that you could expect to occur.

The same approach towards units is adopted as used earlier in the book. In the text, both metric and imperial units are given, but in the tables only the metric values (including all temperatures in degrees Celsius) are given. For those of you who prefer imperial measurements, tables for converting the figures are provided at the end of this appendix (Table A.9).

When you translate the figures provided into the type of conditions you might expect to see in a given area, you need to remember that the mean temperature is the average of the daytime maxima and night-time minima throughout each month. Typically, these maxima and minima are between 3°C (5.4°F) and 5°C (9°F) above and below the mean figure. In addition, the weather will fluctuate during the month about the mean, with spells of mild and cold weather.

To give some impression of what this means in terms of temperature, Fig A.1

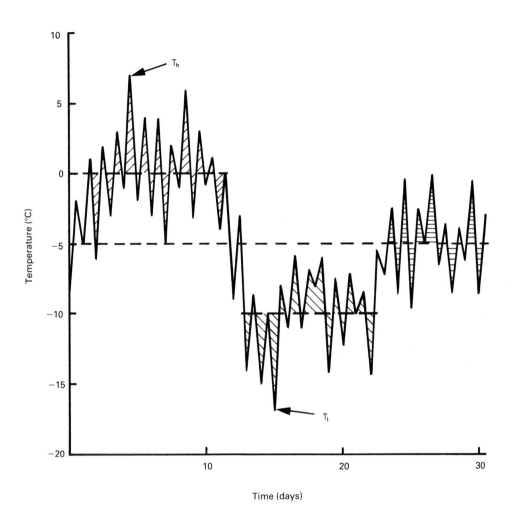

Fig A.1 *A typical temperature record for a mountain resort for a month in midwinter. The trace shows the variations from night to day and from day to day, and demonstrates that even in an average month (mean temperature of −5°C, or 23°F) there can be periods of above-, below- and near -average temperatures. The extremes (T_h and T_l) are the values that might normally be expected during the month (see also Tables A.2–A.8).*

shows a typical monthly record for a site where the average temperature is $-5°C$ (23°F), and the values of T_h and T_l are 7°C (44°F) and $-17°C$ (1°F). Although the average figure over the month is indeed $-5°C$ (23°F), the difference between the first and second ten-day period is striking. During the mild spell (average temperature around freezing), the daytime temperatures are above freezing on several occasions, while during the cold spell (when the mean value was about $-10°C$, or 14°F) they are down to around $-7°C$ (19°F) to $-10°C$ (14°F) – quite a difference. Furthermore, if these are the values in the village, the temperatures are likely to be some 6.5°C (12°F) lower a further 1,000m (3,280ft) up the mountains. So, during the mild spell the conditions will be pleasantly cool, providing it is sunny. But in the cold spell, the temperatures may be between $-15°C$ (5°F) and $-20°C$ ($-4°F$) for much of the day, which is bitterly cold and requires good equipment to keep you warm.

Interpreting the precipitation figures is more difficult. Where the mean monthly temperature is $-3°C$ (27°F) or below, virtually all the precipitation will fall as snow. Where there is more than 50mm (2in) of precipitation in a month, then at these temperatures there is likely to be adequate snow cover in the resort and, because temperatures are lower and precipitation greater at higher levels, considerably more further up the mountain. Where precipitation amounts are less, temperatures need to be a few degrees lower to maintain the snow cover. Where they are greater – say, 100mm (4in) or more – then there will be plentiful snow in the resort for most of the time if the mean temperature is below about $-1°C$ (30°F).

Where available, sunshine figures (S in hours) are also given. As a general guide, more than 100 hours a month in the depths of winter represents a reasonable figure for getting an acceptable amount of time on the slopes. Lower values indicate a frustrating combination of cloudiness and/or short days.

What all this means is that the best conditions of temperature and precipitation at resort level during high season is a mean temperature in the range of -3 to $-7°C$ (27 $-19°F$) and precipitation levels of 50–100mm (2–4in). Lower average temperatures will make the slopes feel bitingly cold, although in such areas these temperatures will make it easier to produce artificial snow and hence improve the runs back to the resort. Similarly, if the monthly precipitation amounts at resort level are well above 100mm (4in), then there will certainly be plenty of snow, but the weather will often be cloudy and stormy. Conversely, as the mean monthly temperature rises above $-3°C$ (27°F) the snow will be liable to increasingly frequent thaws, and heavy precipitation will be needed to maintain a reliable base.

Table A.1

	J	F	M	A	M	J	J	A	S	O	N	D	Yr
				Representative Climatological Data for the Alps								

AUSTRIA

Sonnblick, 47°03′N, 12°57′E (3,106m)

	J	F	M	A	M	J	J	A	S	O	N	D	Yr
T	−13	−13	−11	−8	−4	−1	2	1	0	−4	−8	−11	
T_h	−3	−3	−2	0	4	7	10	10	7	4	0	−2	
T_l	−26	−25	−22	−19	−14	−9	−7	−7	−10	−15	−19	−23	
p	115	108	112	153	136	142	154	134	104	118	108	111	1,495mm
S	109	118	147	139	148	150	167	165	161	147	112	108	1,691hr

Schmittehohe, 47°N, 12°44′E (1,904m)

	J	F	M	A	M	J	J	A	S	O	N	D	Yr
T	−6	−6	−4	−1	4	7	9	9	7	3	−2	−5	
p	115	98	102	118	128	160	183	163	111	91	93	98	1,459mm

Vent, 46°52′N, 10°56′E (1,892m)

	J	F	M	A	M	J	J	A	S	O	N	D	Yr
T	−7	−6	−2	2	5	8	10	10	8	3	−3	−6	
p	41	40	43	49	65	77	89	92	64	54	49	43	706mm

St Anton, 47°08′N, 10°16′E (1,307m)

	J	F	M	A	M	J	J	A	S	O	N	D	Yr
T	−5	−3	0	4	9	13	14	13	11	6	0	−4	
p	81	61	66	71	73	127	149	155	99	78	77	82	1,119mm

Innsbruck, 47°16′N, 11°24′E (582m)

	J	F	M	A	M	J	J	A	S	O	N	D	Yr
T	−3	0	5	9	14	17	18	17	15	9	3	1	
p	57	52	43	55	77	114	140	113	84	71	57	48	911mm
S	73	105	158	166	189	190	210	199	177	145	86	68	1,766hr

GERMANY

Zugspitze, 47°25′N, 10°59′E (2,962m)

	J	F	M	A	M	J	J	A	S	O	N	D	Yr
T	−12	−12	−10	−7	−2	0	2	2	1	−3	−7	−10	
T_h	−2	−2	0	2	7	11	13	12	10	6	1	1	
T_l	−23	−23	−20	−18	−12	−8	−5	−6	−9	−14	−17	−21	
p	203	165	160	178	168	201	210	144	115	129	121	153	1,948mm
S	116	120	164	163	170	136	167	171	178	176	136	118	1,815hr

SWITZERLAND

Säntis, 47°15′N, 9°21′E (2,496m)

	J	F	M	A	M	J	J	A	S	O	N	D	Yr
T	−9	−9	−7	−4	0	4	6	6	4	−1	−4	−8	
T_h	0	0	2	5	10	13	16	15	13	8	4	1	
T_l	−20	−20	−17	−14	−10	−5	−3	−2	−6	−11	−14	−18	
p	202	180	164	166	197	249	302	278	208	183	190	169	2,488mm
S	112	123	166	160	184	174	196	186	170	163	129	117	1,880hr

St Gotthard, 46°33′N, 8°34′E (2,095m)

	J	F	M	A	M	J	J	A	S	O	N	D	Yr
T	−7	−7	−5	−2	2	5	8	8	5	1	−4	−7	
p	185	186	178	209	211	172	167	206	202	232	210	169	2,327mm

	J	F	M	A	M	J	J	A	S	O	N	D	Yr
SWITZERLAND (cont)													
				Bever, 46°53′N, 9°53′E (1,700m)									
T	−9	−8	−4	1	6	10	11	11	7	3	−3	−8	
p	40	43	63	60	77	86	103	107	76	88	73	61	879mm
				Andermatt, 46°38′N, 9°26′E (1,442m)									
T	−6	−5	−1	2	7	10	12	11	8	4	−1	−5	
p	109	93	118	132	125	125	136	133	112	138	114	113	1,448mm
				Geneva, 46°12′N, 6°09′E (405m)									
T	1	2	6	10	14	18	20	19	16	10	6	2	
p	63	56	55	51	67	89	64	94	99	72	83	59	852mm
S	54	98	167	204	236	261	287	257	189	123	61	42	1,979hr
FRANCE													
				Pralognan-la-Vanoise, 45°23′N, 6°23′E (1,480m)									
T	−4	−2	1	4	8	12	14	13	11	6	1	−3	
p	102	93	66	69	90	110	98	108	105	92	86	84	1,102mm
				Lus-la-Croix-Haute, 44°41′N, 5°42′E (1,037m)									
T	−1	0	3	6	10	13	16	15	13	8	3	0	
T_H	15	20	21	24	26	31	32	32	29	28	20	16	
T_L	−21	−23	−18	−13	−5	−2	2	2	−3	−6	−14	−21	
p	86	92	90	81	100	95	53	69	87	121	107	92	1,070mm
				Bourg-St-Maurice, 45°37′N, 5°42′E (865m)									
T	0	1	5	8	12	16	18	17	15	10	4	0	
T_H	14	21	23	26	29	34	35	34	31	26	21	16	
T_L	−19	−19	−15	−8	−2	1	3	4	−1	−5	−13	−18	
p	94	103	72	55	58	78	81	87	63	63	91	108	952mm
ITALY													
				San Martino Castro, 46°16′N, 11°44′E (1,444m)									
T	−4	−2	1	4	8	11	13	13	10	6	1	−2	
p	57	63	60	102	153	166	160	147	130	125	124	70	1,351mm
SLOVENIA													
				Kranjskagora, 46°29′N, 13°47′E (812m)									
T	−4	−3	1	6	11	15	16	16	12	7	3	4	
p	106	105	153	172	170	165	146	176	188	231	279	142	2,035mm

Temperature and Precipitation Values for Ben Nevis (56°48′N, 5°00′W, 1,343m)												
	J	**F**	**M**	**A**	**M**	**J**	**J**	**A**	**S**	**O**	**N**	**D**	**Yr**
T	−4.4	−4.6	−4.4	−2.4	0.6	4.3	5.1	4.7	3.3	−0.3	−1.7	−3.8	
T$_H$	9.1	7.8	7.8	11.4	13.3	19.1	17.8	17.5	17.0	14.0	11.1	7.2	
T$_L$	−17.4	−16.8	−14.7	−11.5	−9.8	−5.1	−3.2	−2.8	−7.6	−9.8	−12.1	−13.8	
p	466	344	387	215	201	192	274	339	400	392	390	484	4,084mm

Table A.2

Representative Climatological Data for the Pyrenees												
	J	**F**	**M**	**A**	**M**	**J**	**J**	**A**	**S**	**O**	**N**	**D**	**Yr**
Bansol, Andorra, 42°35′N, 1°38′W (1,667m)												
T	−1	0	3	5	7	11	15	14	12	8	3	−1	
p	50	54	47	80	107	96	50	94	92	68	67	63	873mm
Pic du Midi, France, 42°56′N, 0°09′E (2,883m)												
T	−7	−8	−6	−5	−1	3	7	6	4	0	−4	−6	
T$_H$	10	10	10	11	15	19	19	20	18	15	12	8	
T$_L$	−27	−33	−23	−21	−15	−11	−8	−8	−11	−18	−21	−25	
p	106	82	86	86	66	59	53	62	63	67	89	107	925mm

Table A.3

	J	F	M	A	M	J	J	A	S	O	N	D	Yr
\multicolumn{14}{c}{Climatological Data for Parts of Europe}													

Climatological Data for Parts of Europe

	J	F	M	A	M	J	J	A	S	O	N	D	Yr
Lillehammer, Norway, 61°06′N, 10°29′E (226m)													
T	−8	−6	−2	3	8	13	16	14	9	4	−2	−6	
p	45	31	25	41	42	78	101	84	71	64	63	59	703mm
Gielo, Norway, 60°32′N, 8°10′E (841m)													
T	−7	−6	−4	−1	5	9	12	10	6	2	−3	−6	
p	54	45	32	36	41	65	87	82	74	68	59	57	699mm
Bergen, Norway, 60°24′N, 5°19′E (44m)													
T	2	1	3	6	10	13	15	15	12	8	6	3	
p	179	139	109	140	83	126	141	167	228	236	207	203	1,958mm
S	22	54	127	142	191	175	165	132	103	69	29	13	1,224hr
Poprad, Slovakia, 49°04′N, 20°15′E (707m)													
T	−6	−4	0	6	10	14	16	15	12	6	1	−3	
p	28	25	34	34	68	85	90	78	43	42	48	33	608mm
S	94	112	169	189	231	231	255	241	208	156	85	81	2,052hr
Sniezka, Poland, 50°44′N, 15°44′E (1,603m)													
T	−8	−7	−3	−2	3	7	9	9	6	2	−2	−4	
T_h	3	4	5	8	14	17	18	18	16	12	8	5	
T_l	−19	−19	−15	−12	−7	−2	1	1	−4	−8	−12	−16	
p	122	94	102	115	127	107	182	140	106	126	100	199	1,440mm
S	66	88	117	119	176	182	161	160	138	104	69	63	1,443hr
Brasov, Romania, 45°39′N, 25°36′E (560m)													
T	−4	−2	3	9	13	16	18	17	13	8	3	−2	
p	35	28	39	59	89	125	101	87	63	51	33	38	747mm
Sofia, Bulgaria, 42°49′N, 25°36′E (560m)													
T	−2	1	5	10	15	19	21	21	17	11	6	1	
T_h	9	12	20	24	27	31	33	32	29	25	18	12	
T_l	−11	−12	−7	−1	4	8	11	10	5	−1	−4	−11	
p	42	31	37	55	71	90	59	43	42	55	52	44	622mm
S	53	89	128	179	226	268	320	296	222	145	78	42	2,046hr
Erzurum, Turkey, 39°55′N, 41°16′E (1,863m)													
T	−9	−7	−3	5	11	15	19	20	15	9	2	−6	
T_h	3	4	9	18	23	27	31	31	28	22	15	7	
T_l	−24	−22	−18	−9	−1	3	7	7	1	−3	−11	−19	
p	29	32	41	53	78	55	31	19	27	49	38	25	476mm
S	105	136	158	198	257	318	363	347	285	236	156	115	2,677hr

Table A.4

Representative Climatological Data for the Rocky Mountains

	J	F	M	A	M	J	J	A	S	O	N	D	Yr
Crested Butte, CO, 36°52′N, 106°58′W (2,703m)													
T	−11	−9	−5	1	7	11	14	13	9	4	−4	−8	
p	71	61	61	44	33	36	52	55	50	34	37	54	588mm
Aspen, CO, 39°11′N, 106°58′W (2,260m)													
T	−7	−5	−2	4	9	13	17	16	12	7	−1	−5	
p	45	46	46	44	39	27	38	41	36	37	34	38	470mm
Steamboat Springs, CO, 40°30′N, 106°70′W (2,064m)													
T	−10	−8	−3	4	9	13	16	15	11	6	−2	−8	
p	61	61	56	55	53	37	38	39	41	47	45	61	595mm
Silver Lake Brighton, UT, 40°36′N, 111°35′W (2,652m)													
T	−8	−7	−4	0	5	10	14	14	10	4	−3	−5	
p	127	135	138	102	68	42	35	50	52	76	103	128	1,056mm
Jackson, WY, 43°29′N, 110°46′W (1,904m)													
T	−10	−8	−4	3	8	12	16	15	11	5	−3	−8	
T_L	−46	−42	−36	−21	−11	−7	−4	−8	−10	−17	−33	−45	
p	39	36	33	31	42	34	20	33	34	30	27	39	395mm
Sun Valley, ID, 43°41′N, 114°21′W (1,775m)													
T	−10	−7	−4	3	8	111	15	14	10	5	−3	−7	
p	56	57	36	19	41	36	18	16	21	31	39	57	432mm
Summit, MO, 48°19′N, 113°21′W (1,589m)													
T	−9	−8	−5	1	6	10	14	13	9	4	−3	−6	
p	108	90	80	71	73	94	31	39	64	79	101	109	937mm
Lake Louise, AB, 51°56′N, 116°11′W (1,540m)													
T	−14	−11	−6	0	6	10	12	11	7	2	−7	−11	
p	77	53	43	41	47	58	54	51	47	47	68	98	683mm
Jasper, AB, 52°53′N, 118°05′W (1,059m)													
T	−11	−8	−3	3	9	12	15	14	10	5	−4	−8	
p	34	21	16	23	33	55	50	49	38	29	30	33	409mm
Glacier, Rogers Pass, BC, 51°17′N, 117°31′W (1,323m)													
T	−10	−7	−3	2	5	10	13	13	8	2	−5	−10	
p	235	170	121	82	72	99	86	88	96	141	195	230	1,612mm

Table A.5

	J	F	M	A	M	J	J	A	S	O	N	D	Yr
Representative Climatological Data for Western North America													
Tahoe City, NV, 39°10′N, 120°09′W (1,699m)													
T	−3	−2	0	3	7	12	16	15	12	7	2	−1	
p	155	138	98	55	31	14	7	4	12	41	79	136	769mm
Crater Lake, OR, 42°51′N, 122°08′W (1,974m)													
T	−4	−3	−2	1	5	9	13	13	10	5	1	−2	
T_L	−26	−28	−21	−18	−15	−12	−8	−9	−8	−12	−22	−28	
p	271	211	191	117	81	64	19	16	56	142	201	276	1,692mm
Rainier (Paradise Lodge), WA, 46°47′N, 121°44′W (1,692m)													
T	−3	−3	−2	1	5	7	12	12	9	5	1	−2	
p	378	285	271	163	119	112	43	71	152	274	364	419	2,635mm
Garibaldi, BC, 49°59′N, 123°08′W (381m)													
T	0	1	3	6	10	13	15	15	12	8	4	1	
p	266	199	173	103	72	64	47	58	109	217	251	287	1,846mm
Yakutat, AK, 59°30′N, 139°40′W (9m)													
T	−3	−2	0	3	7	10	12	12	10	6	1	−4	
p	276	208	221	184	203	129	214	277	420	498	407	312	3,348mm
S	59	51	84	81	71	84	90	71	54	50	36	28	758hr

Table A.6

	J	F	M	A	M	J	J	A	S	O	N	D	Yr
Representative Climatological Data for Eastern North America													
Mount Washington, NH, 44°16′N, 71°18′W (1,909m)													
T	−14	−15	−12	−5	2	7	10	9	5	−1	−7	−13	
p	135	134	147	150	149	164	162	168	172	154	169	163	1,867mm
Somerset, VT, 42°58′N, 72°57′W (634m)													
T	−8	−8	−4	3	10	15	17	16	12	7	0	−6	
p	113	97	119	117	113	113	110	103	113	106	125	110	1,340mm
Ste-Agathe-de-Montreal, QUE, 46°03′N, 74°17′W (399m)													
T	−13	−12	−6	2	10	15	17	16	11	5	−2	−10	
p	93	87	95	84	81	101	106	113	103	88	101	112	1,164mm

Table A.7

Climatological Data from Other Parts of the World

	J	F	M	A	M	J	J	A	S	O	N	D	Yr
Leh, Pakistan, 34°09'N, 77°34'E (3,514m)													
T	−8	−6	0	6	10	14	17	17	13	7	1	−5	
T$_h$	3	7	14	18	22	26	28	27	25	20	12	8	
T$_l$	−19	−19	−13	−5	−1	2	6	6	1	−5	−10	−18	
p	12	9	12	7	7	4	16	19	12	7	3	8	116mm
Christo Redentor, Argentina, 32°50'S, 70°05'W (3,832m)													
T	4	4	3	0	−3	−6	−7	−7	−5	−3	−1	2	
Bariloche, Argentina, 41°06'S, 71°10'W (836m)													
T	14	14	12	8	6	4	3	3	5	8	11	13	
p	33	50	57	46	48	45	47	49	38	37	50	49	574mm
S	195	170	167	150	112	102	112	136	144	161	171	180	1,800hr
Hermitage, Mount Cook, New Zealand, 43°43'S, 170°07'E (765m)													
T	13	13	12	8	5	2	1	3	5	8	11	13	
p	477	386	400	442	342	307	241	316	342	438	363	328	4,380mm
Ski Basin, New Zealand, 43°08'S, 171°41'E (1,554m)													
T	9	10	7	5	2	0	−2	−1	0	3	5	7	
p	138	116	132	177	165	84	34	97	115	139	181	155	1,533mm
Lake Tekapo, New Zealand, 44°00'S, 170°29'E (683m)													
T	16	15	13	10	6	3	2	4	8	10	12	14	
p	53	46	41	48	46	36	41	41	53	56	46	58	564mm
Manorburn Dam, New Zealand, 45°22'S, 169°36'E (746m)													
T	12	12	10	7	4	1	−1	1	4	7	9	11	
p	48	43	36	41	33	25	18	18	23	38	41	43	406mm
Thredbo (Crackenback Station), Australia, 36°29'S, 148°17'E (1,957m)													
T	11	12	9	5	2	−1	−3	−2	0	3	6	9	
p	103	92	124	118	141	101	136	151	175	184	162	111	1,598mm
Tajima, Japan, 37°12'N, 139°46'E (560m)													
T	−3	−2	2	8	14	18	22	22	19	12	6	1	
p	119	85	74	73	76	126	176	170	148	122	70	106	1,352mm
Rusutsu, Japan, 42°44'N, 140°53'E (374m)													
T	−8	−7	−2	4	10	15	18	21	16	9	2	−5	
p	152	87	75	81	78	90	105	126	138	121	126	128	1,318mm

Table A.8

105

Conversion Table					
ALTITUDE		**SNOW DEPTH/SNOWFALL**		**TEMPERATURE**	
(m)	(ft)	(cm)	(in)	(°C)	(°F)
500	1,640	10	4	−40	−40
1,000	3,281	20	8	−35	−31
1,500	4,921	50	20	−30	−22
2,000	6,562	100	39	−25	−13
2,500	8,202	150	59	−20	−4
3,000	9,843	200	79	−15	5
3,500	11,483	250	98	−10	14
4,000	13,124	300	118	−5	23
		500	187	0	32
		750	296	5	41
		1,000	394	10	50
		1,500	591	15	59
				20	68

Table A.9

Glossary

Anticyclone A region where the surface atmospheric pressure is high relative to its surroundings. Often called a 'high', it produces clear, calm weather near its centre, especially at high altitudes in mountainous areas.

Blizzard A term originally applied to the combination of intensely cold gale-force winds and fine drifting snow associated with the passage of some winter depressions across the United States. Now used to describe the combination of high winds, low temperatures and heavy snowfall.

Blocking A phenomenon, often associated with stationary high-pressure systems in the mid-latitudes of the northern hemisphere, which produces periods of abnormal weather.

Breathability The capacity of a fabric to allow perspiration vapour to be transmitted away from the body over a specific period (measured in g/m^2). Fabrics which score over 7,200g/m^2 in twenty-four hours are called ultrabreathable.

Chinook A warm, dry wind, similar to the föhn (*see also* **Föhn**), which occurs on the eastern side of the Rocky Mountains. Blowing from the west, it usually produces a sudden rise in temperature and a subsequent rapid thaw of lying snow.

Cold front The boundary line between advancing cold air and warm air, which the cold air pushes up like a wedge.

Depression A part of the atmosphere where the surface pressure is lower than the surrounding parts; often called a 'low'.

Depth hoar Recrystallized snow which often forms at the interface between layers of snow of different ages. It can greatly weaken the bonds between these snow layers.

Dry adiabatic lapse rate (DALR) The lapse rate which applies to moist air that remains unsaturated. Its magnitude is 9.8°C per km (5.4°F per 1,000ft).

El Niño Southern Oscillation (ENSO) A quasi-periodic occurrence when large-scale abnormal pressure and sea-surface temperature patterns become established across the tropical Pacific.

Firn The German word meaning old snow which is in the process of being transformed into glacier ice.

Föhn A warm, dry wind which blows down the leeward side of a mountain range; best known on the northern slopes of the Alps.

Freezing rain Rain falling from warmer air through colder air that becomes supercooled and then freezes on impact with any surfaces it hits, covering them with clear ice.

Greenhouse effect The trapping by certain atmospheric gases (principally carbon dioxide and water vapour) of the long-wave radiation emitted by the Earth, which leads to the temperature of the Earth's surface being considerably higher than it would otherwise be.

Infra-red Electromagnetic radiation lying between the visible and microwave regions of the spectrum.

Insolation The amount of solar radiation reaching any particular part of the Earth's surface.

Insulation (thermal) The capacity of any material to transmit heat, which in the case of clothing should be as low as possible.

Inversion A reversal of the normal condition when the temperature of the air decreases with increasing height, instead increasing with height in the lower levels of the atmosphere.

Jet stream Strong winds in the upper atmosphere whose course is related to major weather systems in the lower atmosphere, and which tend to define the movement of these systems.

Katabatic wind A wind created when very cold air forms in upland areas and becomes sufficiently dense to drain downhill.

Lapse rate The fall in temperature in unit height, expressed as a positive value. In average conditions in the atmosphere the rate is 6.5°C per km (3.6°F per 1,000ft) (*see also* **Dry adiabatic lapse rate** and **Saturated adiabatic lapse rate**).

Little Ice Age A cooler period in the Earth's climate, usually reckoned to have lasted from around AD1500 to 1850.

Metamorphosis A pronounced change of form and structure that takes place in a comparatively short time; in the case of snow, it reduces snowflakes into amorphous granules.

Ozone A form of oxygen (O_3) created by photochemical action in the upper atmosphere.

Reflectivity The proportion of incident solar radiation returned by a surface.

Saturated adiabatic lapse rate (SALR) The lapse rate which applies to moist air that is saturated. Its magnitude depends on the amount of vapour that is being condensed out of the air as it rises, but in mid-latitudes it is typically 5°C per km (2.7°F per 1,000ft).

Stevenson Shelter A standard housing for ground-level meteorological instruments that is designed to ensure that reliable shade temperatures are measured.

Stratosphere The portion of the atmosphere, typically at an altitude of 12–40 km (7.5–25 miles), where the temperature is approximately constant and there is little or no vertical mixing.

Terminal moraine Irregular ridges of debris representing the furthest extent to which material has been pushed along by a glacier. Lateral moraines are found alongside present and former glaciers.

Ultraviolet (UV) radiation Electromagnetic radiation lying between the visible and X-ray regions of the spectrum. In terms of skin protection, the important parts of this wavelength range are UVA (400–320nm), which tans, and UVB (320–290nm), which burns.

Verglas A clear, wafer-thin layer of ice which makes rocks treacherous and which is a product of either freeze/thaw cycles or freezing rain.

Warm front The boundary line between advancing warm air and the mass of colder air over which it rises.

Warm sector A body of warm air which, in the early stages of the life of many depressions in temperate latitudes, is used up as the system deepens and the cold front catches up the warm front.

Water-resistance A measure of the ability of a fabric to withstand hydrostatic pressure (measured in mm). Functional materials can withstand 450mm, while the best fabrics can hold back more than 10,000mm.

Wicking The ability of fabrics (usually used in the lining of garments) to draw perspiration away from the skin.

Windproofing The extent to which a fabric permits air to pass through it (measured in $cm^3/cm^2/sec$). The value for 100 per cent windproof garments should be 0 $cm^3/cm^2/sec$.

Further Reading

METEOROLOGY

Barry, RG, *Mountain Weather and Climate*, 2nd edition (Routledge, 1992).
If you really want to sink your teeth into the physics and geography of mountain weather, this is the book for you. Not always an easy read, but it provides not only all the basic information about what governs conditions in the mountains, but also copious references which enable you to get to grips with particular aspects of these issues.

Barry, RG and Chorley, RJ, *Atmosphere, Weather and Climate* (Routledge, 1988).
The fifth edition of a well-established, widely read standard work which provides a thorough treatment of current meteorological and climatological knowledge at the right level to put into context the areas described in this book.

Burroughs, WJ, *Watching the World's Weather* (Cambridge University Press, 1991).
This book describes how weather satellites have altered our perspective of the weather and transformed the science of meteorology. It covers a wide range of weather and climate issues, but is of particular relevance here in giving guidance on how to interpret satellite imagery.

Burroughs, WJ, *Weather Cycles: Real or Imaginary?* (Cambridge University Press, 1992).
This book describes the unresolved debate on the existence of weather cycles, presenting the evidence for cycles.

Pedgley, D, *Mountain Weather; A Practical Guide for Hillwalkers and Climbers in the British Isles* (Cicerone, 1979).
This small book delivers precisely what it promises. It is packed with practical information on weather conditions in upland Britain and explains how to relate these to published weather maps; there is relatively little emphasis on the more extreme winter conditions.

Scorer, R and Verkaik, A, *Spacious Skies* (David & Charles, 1989).
An excellent text for viewing many aspects of the weather from a different perspective. It contains a combination of illuminating satellite images and spectacular cloud photographs which, together with an eclectic text, provide many new insights.

CLIMATE CHANGE

Grove, JM, *The Little Ice Age* (Methuen, 1988).
This scholarly work explores the evidence for the colder climate between the 16th and 19th centuries in terms of the historic and other evidence of the expansion and contraction of glaciers around the world. As such, it provides both a fascinating insight into how the climate in the mountains has changed in recent centuries and an unrivalled source of facts that not many other skiers will know.

Lamb, HH, *Climate – Present, Past and Future, Vols 1 and 2* (Methuen, 1972 and 1977).

The classic work on all aspects of climate change, which considers the complete range of meteorology, climatology, the evidence of climatic change and possible explanations for observed changes. Although the subject has moved on a bit since these books were written, they are still the best place to start if you want to know more about climate change.

MOUNTAIN SAFETY

Barry, J, *Alpine Climbing* (Crowood, 1988).

A climbing book with a limited amount of weather information, but with a good section on hillwalking and associated safety. Also has a comprehensive discussion on avalanche hazards and related safety issues.

Birkett, B, *The Hillwalker's Manual* (Cicerone, 1993).

A thorough guide covering such basics as equipment, navigation, route planning and survival for hillwalkers in the British Isles. Little information on weather and still less on winter weather.

Cliff, P, *Ski Mountaineering* (Unwin Hyman, 1987).

A practical guide to high-altitude skiing and ski extreme, covering equipment and technique. There is a good section on avalanches and a useful guide to the best-known high-level tours around the world.

Daffern, T, *Avalanche Safety for Skiers and Climbers* (Diadem Books, 1983).

Probably the best-known and most widely used guide on snow and avalanche safety. If you really want to find out more about the subject, this is where to start. By the time you have mastered the contents of this book, you should be in no doubt whatsoever about the fickle and complex nature of snow in the mountains.

Walker, K, *Mountain Hazards* (Constable, 1988).

Good coverage of safety and weather factors in upland areas of the British Isles. Simple, direct presentation gets important messages across effectively.

RESORT GUIDES

Hardy, P and Eyston, F, *The Good Skiing Guide 1994* (Consumers' Association, 1993).

The definitive guide to ski resorts, covering not only all the major European resorts but also the best-known North American resorts, together with details of some other parts of the world. While short on meteorological data, provides detailed maps of resorts and so complements the information in this book.

Gill, C & Watts, D, *Where to Ski: the up-to-date guide* (Boxtree, 1994).

The latest guide to ski resorts around the world, with the principal emphasis on Europe. The aim is to provide the most comprehensive guide to skiers, including details of snow reliability. It succeeds in supplying a huge amount of the latest information about most aspects of each resort, but the guidance on meteorology is limited. So, as with other guides, it complements the information in this book.

Leocha, CA, *Ski America 1993* (World Leisure Corporation, 1993).

This annual publication has become the classic guide to North American ski resorts. While it contains a great deal about all aspects of the best resorts, it is decidedly thin on the meteorological conditions, so it complements rather than overlaps the information provided in this book.

Index